I'VE GOT
YOUR BACK

"When is the last time you've read a book on follower abuse? I'll bet never. Jim Galvin explores this elephant-in-the-room leadership sin with thoughtfulness, insight and creativity. Leadership—the God-honoring flavor—cannot be learned on a diet of tweets, blog and business books. Jim reminds us that leadership began in the mind of God, but leaders are sinners too. *I've Got Your Back* is brilliant: a page-turner story with a one-of-a-kind section on the theology of leadership and followership. It's the perfect tool for young leaders and their coaches and mentors."

John Pearson, Board Governance and Management Consultant, John Pearson Associates, Inc.

"Jim Galvin has given leaders and followers, thus all the people of God, a wonderfully clear account of what it means to lead and to follow. Until you learn to follow you cannot lead and unless you learn to intentionally follow Jesus your leadership will never have the grace that makes it all work as God intended. This is a well-conceived, practical, and much-needed book. It is not just for designated leaders but for all who truly want to be better disciples."

John H. Armstrong, President, ACT 3 and Author of *Your Church Is Too Small*

"Over the years Jim Galvin has become a personal friend and mentor who has shaped my own leadership in many ways. Any time I'm around him or read anything he's written it's guaranteed to stretch my thinking. In *I've Got Your Back*, Jim has done it again. His clear description of biblical followership and leadership has given me fresh insights not only into the way I lead, but also in the way I follow. I can't wait to put this book into the hands of young leaders!"

Mac Lake, Chief Launch Officer, LAUNCH

"A very creative, captivating insight into the perpetually intriguing subject of leadership. Convincingly connects the twin dynamics of following and leading, and effectively blends time-tested leadership principles with biblically sound theology. This book will stimulate the thinking of every reader."

Paul D. Robbins, President/Publisher (retired), Christianity Today International

"Emerging from years and years of experience in successfully advising and helping others to understand the complex and subtle dynamics of leadership comes *I've Got Your Back*: a veritable manual of practical and biblically solid insights on how to offer our best to build the Kingdom. Study this book and sit at the feet of one of the masters."

Fr. Robert A. Sirico, President, The Acton Institute

"Creative. Foundational. Biblical leadership starts with being a good follower. Jim Galvin knows how to connect Scripture to practical living as good followers. I found myself grading my life on how well I do as a follower. You will, too! Every leader needs to understand what Galvin has unpacked for us."

Robert C. Andringa, Ph.D., President Emeritus, Council for Christian Colleges & Universities

"The available books on leadership are wearingly, never-ending. This book however, finally explains, from a crisply written Biblical perspective, the forgotten issue of how you and I are to follow. No matter how many you think you lead, or hope to lead, you follow. Read it, be convicted, and pass it on to those you equip."

ML. Hillard, Sr.Executive V.P., Peter F. Drucker Academy, Beijing

"Leadership books, or opinions, for that matter, are easy to come by. And I've collected my fair share. But Jim Galvin has written a treasure here, an easy-to-read book that fuses biblical faithfulness with the best insights about what makes leadership work. It drips with wisdom and is as thorough as might be expected from Jim's lifetime of leadership consulting. Already I'm dreaming about how to use it with my family, in my church and with my Youth for Christ colleagues. As for teaching ministry students...I've already figured out which course it will anchor!"

Dave Rahn, Ph.D., Senior V.P. and Chief Ministry Officer, Youth for Christ/USA, and Director, Huntington University's MA in Youth Ministry Leadership

"Thank you, Jim Galvin, for cutting through the cultural influences around Christian leadership. You bring the truth out so clearly for true followers who aspire to be leaders, and for leaders who want to build true followers! Your book is a welcome addition to my toolbox and one that I will use often."

Andrea Buczynski, Vice President, Global Leadership Development, Campus Crusade for Christ

"The final chapter does a masterful job of providing a theology of leadership. This is a theology born out of careful thought about his experience of leadership and the teachings of Scripture. I deeply appreciate the way Jim Galvin acknowledges the tensions in leadership and followership. Often books in this area get one dimension right, but in doing so fail to provide an adequate big picture. He provides a very helpful vocabulary for understanding the call to leadership and followership."

James C. Wilhoit, Ph.D., Scripture Press Professor of Christian Education, Wheaton College

"It's a Biblical principle: everyone has eyes, but many people cannot see. We're all surrounded with leadership, but most people don't know what it looks like. God has given Jim Galvin the perspective to see and understand what real leadership looks like, and has given him the ability to describe it to others. Though I've been leading—and, mentoring leaders—for decades, I've gained new insights from Jim's fresh treatment of truth in *I've Got Your Back*. Any leader worth his or her salt will benefit from this concise consideration of the kind of leadership God honors."

Bob Shank, Founder/CEO, The Master's Program

"Amid the overwhelming volume of information and insights that have flooded the marketplace, here comes a book that masterfully portrays the essence of leadership in the context of a biblical worldview. This couldn't be more timely and refreshing in a world yearning for trustworthy leadership and when leaders seem so often to demean, defraud, and disappoint those who follow. I highly recommend *I've Got Your Back* as a very practical, relevant, and exciting approach to leadership that makes a difference."

Ron Nikkel, President/CEO, Prison Fellowship International

"At the heart of the engaging stories and relatable characters that frame this book is the clearest, most direct analysis of why so many of today's young adults are disillusioned about leadership. Jim Galvin speaks sensitively to the experience of 'follower abuse' that has discouraged our 'best and brightest' from seeking leadership. More important, he challenges them to grow into leadership – not by the traditional 'try harder' path, but rather by becoming better people. In this, Jim captures the essential truth about authentic leadership – it is rooted in a deep understanding of, and commitment to, followership. Every young adult needs to read this book, accept its challenge, and become the followers and leaders we so desperately need."

Peter O'Donnell, President, Healthy Futures Group

I'VE GOT YOUR BACK

A LEADERSHIP PARABLE

BIBLICAL PRINCIPLES FOR LEADING AND FOLLOWING WELL

JAMES C. GALVIN

TENTH
POWER

Elgin, IL • Tyler, TX

TENTHPOWERPUBLISHING
www.tenthpowerpublishing.com

Produced by Fluency

Design by Inkwell Creative

ISBN 978-1-938840-01-2

10 9 8 7 6 5 4 3 2 1

To Paul Robbins
A mentor, friend, and leader worth following

TABLE OF CONTENTS

FOREWORD

I got my first lesson in leadership from Jim Galvin over 30 years ago. I was a high school senior, visiting Wheaton College where Jim was already attending. He had been the number one player on the college tennis team, which I was hoping to join. But the year before I arrived, another tennis player had entered the school who took over the number one role. Tennis players can be pretty competitive about their rung on their ladder. What I saw in Jim was both a fiercely joyful spirit of competition and a humble welcoming of any players who could help the team. He led by both his competence and his heart. He made the rest of us want to be not just better players, but better people. He made us want to mirror his attitude.

It's striking to me how much of this book unpacks the spirit of leadership that Jim himself incarnated all those years ago. Leadership has deep spiritual implications because it speaks to the whole notion of what the Bible calls 'dominion'; an essential part of our being made in the image of God. Every single human being was made to exercise dominion. That means—whether or not someone has the spiritual gift of leadership—the topic of leading and following well is critical to humanity.

And as Jim demonstrates, good leadership is intrinsically connected to good followership. In fact, in many ways, leadership is really a particular form of followership. When it happens best, it leads to flourishing of all involved. One of the great learning labs of this for me was getting married to someone with such strong leadership gifts. My own conviction is that marriage works best when both husbands and wives equally serve and lead out of their giftedness and discipleship.

Another wonderful emphasis of Jim's is that we have not only great teaching about leaders and followers, but a splendidly-led universe through a gracious God, and a shining example of what leadership looks like among humanity in the person of Jesus. But taking Jesus-inspired leadership down to the level of work and ministry and relationships is a whole other challenge.

John Ortberg
Author and Senior Pastor at Menlo Park Presbyterian Church

Leadership is the ability to create a way for people to contribute to make something extraordinary happen. So simply by its own definition, a leader has his or her eyes on others. Servant leadership requires that great leaders develop 'spiritual gift radar,' thinking less about themselves and more about the vision and the people of God. Jim reminds us of this dance between leadership and followership, of being out front as well as behind.

At its best, leadership of any kind—whether it be as a parent, spouse, or boss—divests itself of power in order to invest it in empowering others. The world is hungry for this kind of leadership and our hope is that this book will be one more step in that direction.

Nancy Ortberg
Author of *Non-Linear Leadership*

INTRODUCTION

This book has two parts. The first part is a fictional story of four twenty-somethings who are having major problems with bad bosses. Through the story, you will learn Biblical principles for leading and following well. The second part expands on these principles with more insight and references from the Bible. It is intended to help you develop your theology of leadership.

Writing this has been a ten-year journey for me. In my first attempt, I wrote nine chapters in a popular textbook style. I asked several experts in leadership to read the chapters and offer feedback. They were enthusiastic about the fresh insights and skillful integration of leadership research and Biblical truth. They encouraged me to get it published soon.

Then I showed the chapters to more frontline leaders and younger leaders. The book didn't seem to be doing much for them. After some more thought, I realized that even my own children, who were in college at the time, wouldn't read the book. I had made the classic mistake of writing to my peers instead of the next generation of leaders. So, after years of work, I tore it up to start over.

It took me more than a year to get some traction. How could I get the attention of the next generation who were not interested in leadership positions or learning how to lead? Finally, I hit on the idea of using follower abuse as a starting point and writing the book in a parable format. I went back to my old chapters and selected a few of the best concepts that would be the most useful for helping others build a theology of leadership. I wrote the last section first, and then created the story to engage the next generation of leaders. Perhaps, though, you are still hesitant to tackle a book about the theology of leadership.

Not another book on leadership...

You are right. There are a lot of books about leadership in print. A few years ago, I decided to try to find out how many were being published each year. I did a search on Amazon for a single year of any book covering some aspect of leadership. The number totaled over 1,000 new titles. That means a new book on leadership is released on Amazon every eight hours. Several thousand were released while I wrote this one. The world does not need another mediocre book on leadership. Hopefully, this one will make a lasting contribution.

But I don't like to read fiction...

Some people enjoy getting caught up in a long novel and others do not. Yet, a good story can be powerful. Our brains are wired by God to learn from stories. In the final section of the book, the Biblical principles are taught. In the story, they are caught.

You may wonder if it is a good idea to teach theology using a story. Well, this is exactly what Jesus did when he taught using parables, and he used them all the time.

But I'm not that interested in theology...

Yes, theology can be quite dull and esoteric at times. Sometimes, unfortunately, theology is taught in a boring way. But if you are interested in leading in a way that is God-honoring, then you should be interested in Biblical principles of leadership. If you are trying to apply these Biblical principles, then you are beginning to think theologically about leadership. If the story engages you, then you will not be bored by the theology.

But I don't want to be a leader...

I don't blame you based on the amount of bad leadership we all experience in our lifetimes. But, there is a difference between holding a leadership position and everyday leading and following. Even if you don't want to be a leader in any capacity, you will still remain a follower. This book shows how leading and following are two sides of the same coin. It covers Biblical principles of followership as well as leadership. Everybody needs to learn how to follow well.

How to get more out of this book...

You can read either section first. Some will want to start with the story and others will want to start with the final section. It's not cheating to read the final section first. It's not wrong to only read the story.

Read this book with friends. Your discussion about the story, deeper conversations about how leadership and followership are connected, and dialogue about the theology of leadership will be stimulating and help you go deeper.

Use this book to help next generation leaders gain a secure Biblical foundation for leadership. Many of them have been victims of follower abuse and don't want anything to do with leadership positions. Some of them have issues with authority in their lives and need some guidance to heal. As you mentor them, you will grow as a leader as well.

James C. Galvin, Ed.D.

I'VE GOT
YOUR BACK

1

Wednesday Morning

Jack parked his Jeep Wrangler and walked to the main entrance of the VA hospital. When he arrived at the front desk, the receptionist looked up and said, "How may I help you?"

"I have an appointment with Dr. Carlson," he replied.

She turned and looked down at her computer monitor.

Without looking up she pointed to the left, "Down this hallway, just follow the signs that say Oncology."

Jack proceeded down the hallway. The oncology sign pointed to the left. Instinctively, Jack crouched slightly and glanced to the right before turning left. The next sign pointed him to the right. He looked first to the left while pausing slightly at the intersection, then made the turn and continued walking forward. His movements were so smooth that nobody really noticed this instinctive behavior.

Several nurses were working behind the oncology desk when he walked up. One looked up at him and asked, "Name?"

"Jack Hendrickson."

She went to another counter and picked up a file and a clipboard. "Follow me, please." She took him to an examination room then opened her file. "Last name, first name, middle initial."

"Hendrickson, Jackson, J."

"Birth date and social security number."

He calmly rattled off the numbers.

Then she asked him to step on the scale. "Five foot ten and 182 pounds." She continued by taking his blood pressure and pulse and entering the numbers on the computer. "The doctor will be with you shortly. You can remain dressed."

Soon the door opened. "Hi Jack, good to see you!"

"Good to see you again, doc."

"Have you been feeling well? Any new symptoms developing?"

"I'm good. The Lord is watching over me, doc."

Doctor Carlson asked more general diagnostic questions while scanning his file and looking at several screens on the computer. "Lie down on this table and pull your shirt up if you don't mind."

Jack lay down, unbuttoned his shirt and pulled up his white undershirt.

The doctor began pressing on his stomach to check internal organs. "You're in excellent physical shape. You must be keeping up with your PT."

After listening to his heart and lungs, the doctor put his stethoscope away. "Jack, your numbers all look good. The type of Leukemia you have is treatable and has a 96 percent recovery rate. You are a fortunate man."

"I am blessed by God. But that means a four percent chance of the cancer coming back, right?"

"Jack, let me put this into perspective for you. The copy of your record I have here shows you were in the Army for 20 years. It says you started in the 82nd Airborne Division, graduated with honors from Ranger school, and then attended the Delta Force Assessment and Selection Course. The rest of your record after that is blank after that. I know what that means. You were probably jumping out of black helicopters and conducting raids in really dangerous places."

Jack looked down at his hands, "Yes, I was a soldier for twenty years."

"Jack, listen closely and think carefully about this," Dr. Carlson said. "Your chances of survival are higher now than when you doing special ops. Your chances of survival are higher now than when you were a missionary in Latin America for heaven's sake. You could have been gunned down by a drug lord or kidnapped for a ransom. You traveled through dangerous countries. You're back home now. You're 62. Your prognosis is excellent. You probably have a long retirement or another career ahead of you yet."

"Yeah, I suppose it is safer to stay home and have cancer." Jack hung his head. "I just don't like the idea of sitting around the house recuperating for months and months."

"Jack, look at me. I want you to walk out of this hospital, go home and heal, and then get back to living your life. That's doctor's orders. Hooah?"

"Hooah!" Jack retorted. He jumped up to shake doctor's hand.

RANDALL JOHNSON STOOD BY THE four-wheel cart as he scooped up potatoes from the cardboard box and placed them on the display at the grocery store. Randall was a recent college graduate and had worked in the produce department at Natural Foods for almost two years. He had an athletic build having played soccer in high school. His white apron with the store logo embroidered near the top contrasted with his black skin. His tight haircut and gentle smile made him look more like a store manager than a produce worker.

Looking down the aisle Randall saw his boss Stan approaching. Stan was shorter than Randall, and his stained apron barely covered his protruding stomach. Stan walked fast and with a slight waddle due to knee pain. Randall smiled and nodded as Stan approached.

"Hey dipstick, are you almost done with that? You're not playing Mr. Potato Head over here are you? When you finish with the potatoes, go mop the floor around the lettuce. Be sure to empty the bucket when you're done. And don't let me catch you texting on your phone."

"But I only check messages during breaks." All Randall saw was the backside of Stan as he walked away. "Bye," he said sarcastically as he looked down toward the box of potatoes.

VALERIE MARTINEZ WAS THRILLED TO land a job at Synthetic Software Solutions right out of college. It meant that she had to stay in the Chicago area instead of moving back home to Texas. Valerie was a marketing major and she wanted to get into a fast-growing company with opportunities to move ahead in her career.

She accepted the job of marketing associate with Synthetic only to find out later that most of her work week was spent doing the work of a marketing assistant. She made airline and hotel reservations, handled group scheduling of meetings, and updated the website. Her cubicle walls were four feet high. They were designed so that employees could make eye contact with others when they stood up but would have fewer distractions when seated. The 48 cubicles on her floor were surrounded by offices with doors for the executives and glass-walled meeting rooms. Due to organizational growth, they had moved her cubicle twice in two years.

Valerie had long brown hair that she usually wore straight, large brown eyes, and a slight Latino accent on certain words. She was just as comfortable speaking in Spanish as English. She always saw that as an asset, but Synthetic has no plans to package products for a Spanish-speaking market.

Valerie walked down to the first floor and bumped into her supervisor, Tiffany, who was just going back upstairs after taking a smoke break outside. "Hi Tiffany, do you have minute for a quick question?"

"Sure, kid. What's up?" Tiffany was petite and slender like a model. She always wore fashionable dresses and shoes.

"I just wanted to ask your advice about moving ahead here with my career. I mean, I like what I'm doing, but I'm wondering how I can start doing more marketing work. You know, writing brochure copy, doing a marketing study or something"

Tiffany narrowed her eyes and turned her head slightly to the side while maintaining eye contact. Then she burst out laughing. "Look, kid, let me explain it to you this way. We only have one marketing department here. I'm not going anywhere soon, so that means you're not going anywhere either." Then she glared at her and slowly shook her head in a disapproving way.

BRAD DAVIS WAS FEELING NERVOUS ABOUT meeting with the board chair. He had been on full-time staff with Suburban Life for the past three years. But his executive director recently resigned and now the board was asking him to consider taking this position.

Brad enjoyed youth ministry and he simply wanted to keep doing what he felt God was calling him to do. He majored in communications in college because he enjoyed speaking. Youth ministry was a great fit for him because it allowed him to use his college major and his spiritual gifts. He started out as an education major because he wanted to be a teacher and coach, but switched to communications after his third semester.

Brad was short for a varsity basketball player at five foot ten inches, but he was quick. He still enjoyed playing basketball and working out. The biceps and triceps of his muscular arms tended to stretch out the fabric of his short-sleeve polo shirts. His v-shaped upper body was attached to legs of a sprinter. His blond hair was never combed, although he liked to joke that he worked hard to get it to stick up a different way each day.

Mark Sonnenberg, the board chair finally arrived at the Suburban Life office and warmly greeted him. "Brad! Good to see you. Let's have a seat in the meeting room."

Brad pointed him toward the room and stopped in the back to bring two cups of coffee in small, white Styrofoam cups.

Mark got to the point quickly. "Brad, with Nick leaving we need to find a new executive director, and the board would like to move fast on this. Our first choice is to appoint you to the position. That's the purpose of our meeting today. I'd like nothing better than to walk out of here and announce that to the rest of the staff."

"No, not interested," Brad said apologetically. "I mean, don't say anything to anybody. I didn't come on staff to do fund raising all of the time. I raise my own support so I can do youth ministry. I just want to work with kids. I don't want to be the director."

"Brad, you can still run a club. Let's talk."

"Nick left this place in bad shape. We're $30,000 in debt."

"It's mostly a cash flow issue," Mark replied.

"Mark, we're behind $30,000 in cold, hard cash."

"The board can step up and get us through the temporary cash flow crisis. We can also get access to a line of credit if we need it. The board isn't worried about the financials. What they are worried about is leadership. They don't want to bring in a guy from the business world with no ministry experience like they did with Nick. He was on the board of youth ministry at his church for years, so we thought he could figure out youth evangelism."

Brad's facial expression tightened. "Well you can't figure out youth evangelism by sitting in your office all day."

"Exactly Brad, that's why the board wants you to accept this position. You are our first choice. As a youth worker, you will be able to lead the other youth workers. They will respect you."

"Mark, all five of us are peers. All of the others have been on staff longer than me. I don't want to become their boss all of a sudden."

"Then look at this opportunity as being a leader among equals."

"Try telling them that."

"Brad, this will mean a raise for you of course. People in the community will consider you a leader. Plus, it will look really good on your resume."

"I don't have a resume."

"Brad, will you do the board a favor and just pray about this opportunity for a couple of days?"

LYNETTE CHIANG WAS CHINESE-AMERICAN. Her father was Chinese and her mother was Anglo. Lynn worked at Primary Care Medical Clinic as a billing specialist. Medical coding was complicated to begin with and was made more so by the large percentage of Medicare and Medicaid patients this clinic served. Primary Care had more than 70 family practice physicians, internists, and pediatricians.

Lynn didn't intend to make her mark in the world doing paperwork and filling out forms. She majored in biology and wanted a job in a medical field. But she didn't want to be a nurse and couldn't afford to go to med school. This position was not her first choice but she was grateful to be assisting medical professionals.

Lynn sat in an open office space with seventeen other clerical workers. Dr. Eric Hanson was the clinic director and office manager. He directly oversaw Lynn and all other seventeen people in her department. Lynn had a hard time getting questions answered to be able to do her job. Dr. Hanson would only take questions when he walked out of his office. He didn't want to be disturbed.

As Lynn was working on a billing error, Dr. Hanson opened his door and walked into the 'pit,' as they called their open office space. Three hands shot up. "Lynn, let's start with you. What do you got?"

"I found that we have two codes for the same procedure with different pricing. What should I do?"

"Well, fix it I suppose."

"But doctor, which pricing and technical term should I use?"

"Um, ask around with some of the other doctors. See what they say and get back to me."

Dr. Hanson made the rounds to the other two desks to answer their questions, and then he went back into his office and closed the door. A woman working in payables looked over at her and rolled her eyes. She knew it was another do-it-yourself project for Lynn. The woman walked by and said in a low, quiet voice, "He runs this place like a triage center. One-third of the problems he ignores because they might go away on their own, one-third he ignores because he doesn't know what to do, and one-third he micro-manages from inside his office."

2

Friday Night

The weekly Bible study at Valerie's apartment always began with food. Tonight, it was pizza. Lynn and Valerie sat at the table while Valerie told Lynn about the way Tiffany dumped the latest project on her. Brad and Randall stood by the counter talking about the game coming up on Sunday. All four were recent graduates of Divine Servant University. All four now lived and worked in the Chicago area.

Brad decided to start the Bible study because he felt he needed to spend at least one night a week with people his own age. Using his social networking platform, he got in touch with other graduates living in the area, and four were willing to commit to a small group experience with serious study and discussion. Although they all knew each other at college, they were not close friends then. Now they were becoming closer.

When they were done with pizza and had prayed, Brad started the study. "Okay, we had a good discussion on Romans 12 last week. Tonight we are on Romans 13. I'll read the first paragraph, verses 1-5.

> *Everyone must submit to governing authorities. For all authority comes from God, and those in positions of authority have been placed there by God. So anyone who rebels against authority is rebelling against what*

> *God has instituted, and they will be punished. For the*
> *authorities do not strike fear in people who are doing*
> *right, but in those who are doing wrong. Would you*
> *like to live without fear of the authorities? Do what*
> *is right, and they will honor you. The authorities are*
> *God's servants, sent for your good. But if you are doing*
> *wrong, of course you should be afraid, for they have*
> *the power to punish you. They are God's servants, sent*
> *for the very purpose of punishing those who do what is*
> *wrong. So you must submit to them, not only to avoid*
> *punishment, but also to keep a clear conscience.*

Valerie spoke first, "Well, starting with the first verse, I've got a problem with the word *submit*."

Brad probed, "What's your problem with *submit*?"

"Submit to Tiffany? Are you crazy?"

"But she is your direct supervisor, right?" Lynn asked.

"Lynn, I thought you were on my side," Valerie said with mock disappointment.

"Hey Val, I have to do everything Stan says," said Randall. "You think that's easy?"

Lynn continued, "Every company has people in authority. As employees we need to submit ourselves to their authority. If we don't, then we are bad employees?"

Valerie shook her head, "But this can't mean every authority figure including my seriously flawed supervisor."

"Hold that thought," said Randall as he typed a few words into his computer. "Here is 1 Peter 2:13-14." He read:

> *For the Lord's sake, respect all human authority—*
> *whether the king as head of state, or the officials he has*

*appointed. For the king has sent them to punish those
who do wrong and to honor those who do right.*

"So, I think it means all human authority," said Randall.

"I don't like the way this is going," Valerie said. "This must be one of those difficult verses in the Bible."

Lynn looked over to Brad, "You're being pretty quiet. What do you think?"

"I think I'm feeling sick."

"Why?" Valerie asked.

"I met with our board chair this week and the board wants to make me the next executive director."

"Cool," said Randall.

"Uncool Randall. I don't want to sit in an office. I don't want to spend my time begging people for money. I just want to work with kids."

"Cool," said Randall.

"No Randall, it gets worse. I told them I would pray about it and then promptly put the whole thing out of my head. Now this Bible passage is hitting me right between the eyes. If I am going to submit to those in authority over me, then I need to accept the position. There has to be a way out of this for me."

Valerie asked, "Brad, you hardly know those guys and they don't know you. Are they really in authority over you?"

Randall said, "If they are the board of directors, then they are legally in authority over the entire organization and everyone in it. And, let's see…that would include you."

"I think if you tell the board no, and they are legally in authority over you, then you are being rebellious," Lynn said. "That's not good Brad. As someone working in ministry you should never have a rebellious spirit."

Brad sighed, "Well, now I'm really going to pray about this seriously...praying to get out of it."

"Randall, how does this apply to your situation?" Valerie asked.

"I have to do what Stan tells me. My plan is to get promoted to manager, and then get promoted again to store manager, and then I can tell Stan what to do. He will have to submit to my authority. So I think it will work out over time."

Valerie asked, "So you just do what he says, huh? Lynn, how does this apply for you at work?"

"This passage is plain and straightforward. It says all authority comes from God and those in positions of authority have been placed there by God. I think that is pretty clear. I do what Dr. Hanson tells me do to at work."

"Of course, that's easy for you because he barely talks to you. You are pretty much on your own," Valerie said. "Tiffany is always telling me how to do everything. She wants me to check for flights on one website and buy the ticket on a different one. Everything has to be her way. I have it harder than you do when it comes to submitting to a supervisor at work."

"Yes," said Lynn, "but this passage is not about whether submission is easy or hard, it simply says to submit to authorities. At church, this is exactly what my pastor teaches. The pastor is the spiritual authority in a congregation and the people need to submit to this authority and follow his leadership. Simple."

"But it doesn't mean that we should become sheep. That's taking the passage too far. We shouldn't be submissive employees who creep around with our heads down afraid somebody is going to speak to us," Valerie said.

"The passage says submit to authority, not to become a submissive person," Brad said. "There's a big difference between those two."

Randall added, "I think we can all agree on that. We aren't supposed to be mousy, fearful people. We can also agree that we should obey the laws of the land. But we are all having trouble with the idea of submitting to a bad boss. I think that is what we all have in common here."

"Good clarification," said Brad. "Think back to other bad bosses you have had and how you handled submitting to their authority in the past."

Valerie brushed back her brown hair and said, "I used to waitress at a breakfast restaurant, and the manager would tell us to take unused butter pats off the plates and use them for the next customer. I just ignored him and scraped everything off the plates into the garbage when he wasn't looking."

Randall leaned toward her with mock seriousness, "So you do have a problem with submission."

Valerie smiled. "I'm no militant feminist, but you get ahead in life by taking action, not by being submissive."

"I worked for a landscaping company one summer, and the boss made me ask permission to do everything," said Brad. "One time I saw some leaves near the side of a house so I grabbed the rake to take care of them. He yelled at me for grabbing the rake and gave me a different task. He was a total control freak."

"So did you submit to his authority?" asked Randall.

"Yes, I didn't want an argument. If he got really mad he would start yelling at me in Spanish and some of the other guys would start laughing at me. I didn't know what he was saying. So I ended up just standing around there until he told me what to do next. It felt horrible."

Lynn said, "Well you did the right thing, didn't you?"

"I'm not sure about that at all," Brad said. "I felt like a puppet, but what else was I supposed to do?"

"Don't ask me," said Lynn.

Sunday Morning

Brad got up in the morning and drove to church as usual at Riverview Community Church. Riverview was only about ten years old but had grown quickly to 5,000 people attending worship each weekend. Brad usually sat in the same section of the auditorium, and he and his friend Steve would find each other inside.

The new auditorium held 2,000 people when full. The wall behind the stage held three giant screens for media and a close shot of the pastor preaching the sermon. The worship format was 30 minutes of music followed by 30 minutes of teaching.

Fifteen minutes into the sermon, Steve squeezed Brad's arm. "Dude, wake up. You're going to give yourself whiplash."

"Thanks," Brad whispered.

"Dude, you do this every Sunday. What's your problem?"

"Youth ministry is a demanding career, my friend."

Steve glared at him. "We've got to talk."

LYNN ALWAYS SAT NEAR THE FRONT at New Life, a vibrant charismatic church. New Life had about 1,000 people offering praise to God every weekend. They also had a wide range of recovery groups that met every Tuesday evening on their campus. She was raised in a small Chinese Alliance church but had come to love the praise and worship experience at New Life.

Pastor Howard Smith greeted Lynn between services. "Lynn, do you have a minute to talk? I've sensed that the Lord has been leading me to start a twenty-something ministry here at the church. I think you would be perfect to serve as our first leader. Would you like to launch this new ministry?"

Lynn took a half step backwards, "No, not really. Not at all."

"But why not? You're not involved at church any other way right now. You are a member of this age group. I'm envisioning the group including ages 21 to about 35 or so. What do you think?"

"I don't think I'm gifted for that."

"I know, you haven't had any time at all to think about this. Well please pray about this for a couple of days. And don't forget that Hebrews 13:17 says to obey your spiritual leaders and do what they say. As the spiritual authority in your life, Lynn, I really think you ought to lead this new program."

"Okay," Lynn replied glumly, "I will pray about it."

VALERIE WAS RAISED CATHOLIC AND after visiting a wide range of protestant churches during her college years she had decided to attend Sacred Heart Catholic Church down the street from her apartment. The hard wooden pews and tall stained glass windows felt familiar and gave her a feeling of transcendence in worship that she could find nowhere else.

After mass, Valerie moved to the fellowship area to talk with her priest. "Hi Father O'Brien. I feel like I want to do more for God. I would like to find a meaningful place of service."

"Interesting. Your name is Vicky, right?"

"Close, it's Valerie."

"Oh, okay. Valerie, just keep attending mass regularly and love your neighbor as you love yourself and you will find plenty to keep you busy."

"Well, I was thinking of maybe helping homeless people somehow or helping with a soup kitchen, but I work during the days."

"Well, we don't have any ministries like that in this parish. We are just too small. You know, we could always use some help in the nursery."

"Thank you," said Valerie.

RANDALL WAS ATTENDING FAITH BIBLE Church when they announced their plans to launch a new multi-site location in Hillcrest. Randall signed on as a core volunteer and was assigned to setup and tear-down team. He was pleased to be a part of this exciting new start. They held eight 'soft launch' worship services to work out the kinks before holding their first official worship service in January with 250 people in attendance. Unfortunately, the buzz wore off by summer.

Randall stood staring at the pile of folding chairs lying on the floor. "Look at this mess. I'd get fired at work if my boss saw anything looking like this," he complained to his teammate Tom. "Why is everything so disorganized around here? Our worship attendance is down under 100 now. This site is falling apart."

Tom looked sympathetically at Randall. "Well, you know Pastor Steve is more of a people person than an administrator."

"Yes, he is more of a people person than a preacher. He is more of a people person than a leader, too."

"Ouch!" said Tom softly.

"Well, we ought to do something about this. We can't just let this site fall apart over the summer."

"Do you want to talk to Pastor Steve?"

"That's not going to change anything."

"What do you recommend?" asked Tom.

Randall shook his head, "I just don't know."

Friday Night

When Brad arrived at Valerie's apartment for the small group Bible study, Valerie had her arm around Lynn, who was wiping tears from her eyes. "What's wrong?" he asked.

"Lynn's pastor is pulling the spiritual authority card on her," Valerie said.

"He called me yesterday after work and told me that as the spiritual authority in my life he was instructing me to help start a new singles ministry at the church. I don't want to do that," Lynn said. "I've never led anything like that before."

Brad asked, "Did he hurt your feelings?"

"No," Lynn responded, "It just felt wrong to submit to his authority. Now I'm confused. I have more questions than I did last week."

When Randall arrived, everyone asked how he was doing. "Terrible. Horrible. The store manager called me into his office this morning and told me that the manager position I applied for was going to another co-worker. I didn't even know she was applying for it. I'm older than she is and I've worked there longer."

"Why didn't the store manager pick you?" asked Valerie.

"The co-workers have a big say in our system. The store manager said that my co-workers rated me below average on leadership."

"But you are a good leader," said Lynn.

"Tell that to my co-workers."

They continued talking as they ate pizza. Lynn talked about her boss hiding in his office. Randall told how Stan was complaining about one of the drivers making deliveries and then blurted out, "It's not like I have anything against black people, you know." Valerie told how her supervisor gave her a project to research acrylic racks to hold brochures for the lobby. The next day Tiffany came to her with the research already done and said, "Here, order these." Brad listened attentively as he didn't have a boss to complain about.

Suddenly, Brad looked up excitedly. "Hey, we don't have a submission problem here."

"What do you mean, Brad?" asked Lynn.

"Look, Lynn, if you submit to your pastor it's bad and if you don't submit it's bad, right?"

"I think that sums up my predicament," she replied.

"Randall, you can't really submit to Stan, you only put up with him, yet you can't say no either."

"Correct."

"Valerie, you don't think it would be wise to simply submit to Tiffany."

"So what?" asked Valerie.

"So, we've got a bigger issue here. I don't think our problem is unwillingness to submit to authority, I think it's figuring out how to work for bad bosses and follow bad leaders."

"Go on," said Randall.

"We work for flawed people. Think about it. My board of directors didn't know we had a financial crisis going on and they were surprised when Nick quit. Stan will never get his own store. Tiffany sounds like a piece of work. Your boss, Lynn, is missing in action. What we really need to do is figure out how to work for bad bosses."

"I'm liking this," said Randall, "keep going."

"My church experience is doing fine, but you are all having problems following your leaders. Am I wrong on any of that?" Brad asked.

"I think I would do better with a priest who knew my name," said Valerie.

"So we need help following bad leaders," said Randall. "Now what do we do?"

"I think we need some coaching."

"How are we going to find that?" asked Randall.

"I can't afford to pay for a coach," said Lynn.

"Great," said Valerie, "now we get to submit to a coach too."

"No," Brad said, "I think we should be able to find an older, wiser person to help us think through our dilemmas. Perhaps we could find someone who would be willing to meet with us for free."

"After my meeting this morning, I need to talk to somebody about my job. I need a game plan," said Randall.

"If anybody can help me deal with Tiffany than I'm willing to listen," Valerie added.

"Well if everyone else is up for it then I'll join in too," said Lynn. "But how are we going to find the right mentor?"

"I have an area pastors meeting coming up this week. I'll have to apply some of my 'power networking' for this one," Brad said as he cracked his knuckles.

Wednesday Evening

Everybody met at 7:00 p.m. in the parking lot of Westfield Bible Chapel. Brad brought them up to date.

"I asked a couple of pastors for connections to locate an older, wiser person who would coach the four of us around leadership issues. Pastor Evan Greene said he knew somebody who might be a fit but it would take about a week to get back to me. He called back to set up this meeting. I think we might be meeting the coach tonight. Let's go see."

They went to the church office and the volunteer on duty brought them to Pastor Greene's office. He greeted them cheerfully, "Hi Brad! Good to see you. What special friends did you bring with you tonight?"

They greeted one another and Pastor Greene seated them at a round table. He looked each one of them in the eye then kindly asked, "So tell me why you think you need a mentor?"

Brad spoke for the group. "We want help learning how to work for bad bosses and follow weak leaders. We all have different situations at work and church but we discovered that we share a similar root problem. We thought some coaching could help."

"Interesting," said Pastor Greene. He rested his chin on his hand then said, "How committed are you to listening to this person and doing what he says?"

"We are very committed," said Brad. All four nodded in agreement.

"Well you are going to need to be very committed for the person I have in mind to match up with you all. His name is Jack Hendrickson. He spent twenty years in the Army doing special ops. He was part of a super elite unit called Delta Force. Then he spent twenty years as a Bible translator in Latin America. Currently he has been at home on sick leave. He's feeling better now. He is well-respected by business leaders and ministry leaders alike. He is willing to have one interview with you."

"Why just one meeting?" asked Valerie.

"Because he first wants to find out if you are serious about growing as a leader. Here is my one piece of advice to you for that meeting: Each of you needs to be able to state succinctly the problem you want to solve or the goal you want to achieve. You need to be specific."

"We can work on that," Brad said.

"Then, if he agrees to work with you, do what he says. He was a first sergeant in the Army. Those are the alpha male leaders on the ground.

If he asks you to read a book, have it done before your next meeting. If he assigns you an action project, do it immediately. Don't put it off. I'm warning you, don't waste his time. Oh, and don't be afraid of him either."

Valerie sunk her head into her shoulders, "Sounds like we should be very afraid of this guy."

3

Friday Night

Back in Valerie's apartment, Brad opened the meeting by saying, "Forget the regularly scheduled Bible study. We have to help each other figure out what we want from Jack, and we have to be specific. Randall, why don't you start? What are you going to tell Jack?"

"I need to get better at leadership or I'm going to be working for Stan the rest of my life. How can I be a better leader? How can I get my peers to see me as a leader?"

"Good," said Brad, "How about church?"

"Church is disorganized and people are not coming back. I'm not in charge; I just help with setup and tear down. What can I do when the pastor doesn't want any help?"

"Good," said Brad, "Who's next?"

"Well," said Valerie, "I need to work around Tiffany somehow and figure out how I can get ahead at work. I want to start doing some real marketing work. I need it for my resume. Church is trickier. I can't figure out how to get more connected at my parish and I don't want to go church shopping. I just want to find a meaningful place to serve."

"Nice. How about you, Lynn?"

"My pastor, who is also my spiritual authority, wants me to start a singles ministry, which I don't want to do, so what should I do? I don't have any issues at work."

"Lynn," said Randall, "your boss is worse than mine. Look at all the unnecessary problems you have at work. You can't get answers to your questions. You can't get all the resources you need to do your job."

"Well, yes, I wish someone would come in and help us streamline our systems. That's what we need at work."

"Good," said Brad. "I don't have any problems at church. My number one problem right now is how to get the board off my back without getting them mad at me so I can get on with my ministry. And then I have to make sure they don't hire another guy like Nick. It would be better for us to have no executive director than another bad one."

"That's probably a bigger problem than all of our other problems put together," said Randall.

Sunday Afternoon

They drove together in Lynn's car to the address where Jack was temporarily living. They found a simple ranch home with white siding and black shutters. They walked up to the front door. "Here we go," Brad whispered as he pushed the doorbell.

The door opened and a petite woman with salt and pepper hair smiled at them. "Welcome! I'm Betty, Jack's wife. Please come in." She opened the door wide and closed it behind them.

"Hi Betty, I'm Brad Davis." Brad held out his hand to shake but she kept her hands behind her back and smiled enthusiastically. "This is Randall Johnson, Lynn Chiang, and Valerie Martinez."

"So nice to meet you all!" she said in a caring voice. Then she reached over to a small table and held up a family-sized bottle of anti-bacterial gel. "Hand sanitizer anyone?" She pushed the pump twice for an ample dose for each of them. Brad and Randall exchanged a quick glance.

"Jack is recovering from cancer, you know. The drugs reduce the effectiveness of his immune system, so we take precautions where we can. Jack is finishing up a phone call in the other room but I'll take you to his office now."

As they walked by the first door they caught a glimpse of a man hunched over a cell phone, his head obscured by the shadows. They heard him talking forcefully in a hushed voice, "No! I will not do that! I'm not interested in your reasons either. This conversation is over."

Lynn grabbed Valerie's arm as they nervously walked into Jack's office. They stood quietly and waited for Jack to finish his call. Near the back wall sat an old, gray office desk and an uncomfortable looking chair. A large whiteboard covered most of the side wall. Only one sentence was written on the whiteboard:

Take up your cross and follow me.
(Mark 8:34)

Then Jack walked through the door. He was the same height as Brad, about five foot ten. He had sandy brown hair cut short with a clean-shaven face. He wore dark green cargo pants and a plain white tee shirt. His muscles in his upper body were well-toned with no fat, like a varsity wrestler.

Jack smiled at them. "Welcome to our home. It's so nice to meet you. My name is Jack." He thrust out his hand and all four were still rubbing in the hand sanitizer. "Hah, looks like Betty got you."

After greeting each other, he had them sit at the round table and five chairs set up for them. Jack took orders for water, lemonade, coffee, or tea. He came back with hot water for tea for Lynn and opened a sleek wooden box for her to select a tea bag. Then he came back with serving bowls filled with pretzels and peanuts. "Would anyone like anything else?"

"We're good, Jack," said Brad. "Thank you for your hospitality."

Jack looked at each of them. "Well, let's get acquainted. Tell me where you are from, where you went to school, and what you do for money." Jack clicked his ballpoint pen and prepared to take notes.

After an awkward silence and several glances at each other, Valerie spoke up. "I'm Valerie Martinez. I'm originally from Texas. I went to Divine Servant University and majored in business with a marketing emphasis. I work at Synthetic Software Solutions."

"I'm Lynn Chiang. I went to Divine Servant University and majored in biology. I wanted to work in the medical field but didn't want to be a doctor or nurse. So I work as an admin at Primary Care Medical Clinic."

"I'm Randall Johnson. I'm from the Chicago area and I majored in history at Divine Servant. I work in the produce department at Natural Foods now."

"And I'm Brad Davis. I'm also from the area and majored in communications at Divine Servant. Now I'm on staff with Suburban Life doing youth ministry."

Jack took rapid notes. "So, you were all friends in college?"

"Not really," Randall said, "we knew each other but we didn't really hang out. We got together a few months ago to be in a small group Bible study. Then we got talking about problems we were having at work and decided to find someone who could offer us some life coaching."

"Did you go to college, Jack?" asked Valerie.

"Yes, I completed my Associate's degree in the army then finished my last two years when I got out. I majored in Bible. Then I completed a master's degree in missions."

"Why did you join the army?" Lynn asked.

"Well, because I had a low draft number. I was in the low double digits. I chose to join the army immediately after high school instead of waiting around to get drafted. You had more options if you enlisted."

"We heard you were in special ops!" said Brad.

"I had a ranger tab, that is true."

"What kind of action did you see?"

"I can't tell you about what I did. The law does not permit it. What I can tell you is that I was involved in the invasion of Panama to capture Manuel Noriega. I was in the first wave." He looked down at the table and mumbled, "Actually, a little bit before the first wave."

"Have you ever killed anybody?" Brad asked.

Jack looked straight ahead and with a calm voice said, "Next question."

Valerie spoke to break the tension, "How did you become a missionary?"

"Well, in the army I became fluent in Spanish and I sensed God leading me into Bible translation. After finishing my degree, I applied to serve with Valiant International Mission. They sent me to Peru. VIM does mostly church planting but also some translation work. So I led translation projects the first seven years. Then they made me a regional supervisor and eventually put me in charge of all of their work in Latin America."

"That's an amazing career path," said Randall.

"Well let's focus on you four now. Here's how I work with emerging leaders. You come with a question. I help you answer it. I give you an action assignment. You report back what you learned and bring another question. Clear?"

They nodded in agreement.

"So tell me your dilemma," Jack pointed at himself with his thumb, "and tell me what you want from me."

"I'll start," said Brad. "The board is asking me to serve as the next executive director. My dilemma is that I don't want to take on this role, but I also don't want another bad boss."

"So what do you want from me?" asked Jack staring intently at Brad.

Brad swallowed hard. "I want you to help me figure out how to get the board off my back."

"That was specific," said Jack. "Good. Who's next?"

Valerie sat upright in her chair. "My dilemma is that I'm stuck. I'm stuck at work, at church, and in life. I want you to help me come up with plans for a better future."

"Uh huh," said Jack. "That's actionable."

"My dilemma is that I just got passed over for a promotion," said Randall. "My peers rated me low on leadership. I want a promotion at work."

"You've got to be promotable before you can be promoted," said Jack.

"I want you to show me how to become a better leader."

"Doable," said Jack.

Lynn said, "My dilemma is that I don't know what to say to my boss who won't help me, and I don't know what to say to my pastor who won't listen to me. I want you to help me figure out how to deal with bad leaders."

"Got it," said Jack. "So let me sum up here. We've got some work issues, we've got some ministry issues, and we've got four college graduates ready for some leadership training."

"But I don't want to learn how to lead!" said Lynn. "I don't want to be the boss. I don't want a promotion."

"Yes, of course not," said Jack gently. "But you see, Lynn, the best way to deal with bad leaders is by helping them to lead better. You need to know enough about leadership to show them how to lead you. You need to be a leader yourself in order to deal effectively with a bad leader."

"But I can't do that!" said Lynn in an uncharacteristically loud voice.

"Precisely," Jack said calmly. "You can't. But the strength of your objection shows me that you have what it takes to learn."

Jack looked at the other three. "How do the rest of you feel about learning to lead?"

"I'm all in," Randall said. "I can use this."

"If this applies to leading youth and volunteers, then I'm willing to work hard at it," said Brad.

"I'm excited," added Valerie. "If I want to get any big projects in marketing, then I'm going to have to be able to lead a team. If I get a promotion, then I'll have to know how to work collaboratively with other leaders in the company."

Brad asked, "How long will this process take? What kind of commitment are we talking about here?"

"If Sundays work for all of you, then we'll meet every Sunday afternoon for a couple of months," said Jack.

"When will we be done?" asked Brad.

"When you learn to lead or I get my next assignment, whichever comes first."

"Will your next assignment be with VIM?" asked Valerie.

"No, probably not. They fired me." Jack paused to scan his notes. "So, I think I have a handle on where you all are at and what you need. Are you ready for your first assignment?"

The four sat completely still. "Jack, what do you mean you got fired?" asked Brad.

"Well, just that. They let me go. But I don't want to bore you with the challenges I'm facing. We're here to work on your issues."

Brad leaned forward and said, "Mr. Hendrickson, we have to know more about this before we can agree to be coached by you. Why were you fired by a ministry?"

"Well, because you insist, let me give you some background so this will make sense to you. VIM doesn't have many translators so we all did our training with Wycliffe. I was assigned to Peru. I shipped off to Lima and waited there to meet up with my field supervisor. He took me to meet some contacts in five different people groups who lived in the high plateau region. After returning to Lima he took me to a place where we could see the mountains. He passionately shared with me his vision to see completed New Testaments for all five of those people groups in the next 35 years. He told me that, because I was the first one in line, I could choose whichever group I felt the most affinity with. Then he left. I was to visit the five people groups again, make my choice, and move there.

"When I traveled up there with Betty, I met with our contacts and they asked me to bring some items to their children who were in University or working in Lima. When I delivered the gifts, I also invited them over the following Sunday for lunch. That's how I got to know the young leaders in Lima. As I sat with them and kept thinking about the vision of five New Testaments I wondered, why not do all five translations at once? If these young leaders would join me in the task, then the vision could be done in seven years instead of 35."

"Wow, I'll bet your supervisor was impressed," said Brad.

"No, he was livid. His vision was to have five different translators each complete one translation. He had been a translator himself and he made it clear that getting young people to assist was not the way translation was properly done. One had to live with the people and personally translate it all to guarantee the work was accurate. He told me to choose one people group and move out of Lima.

"When I broke the news to the young leaders, they were upset. They saw great value in working to preserve their heart language. So I challenged them to recruit five small teams who would each take on their own language. They quickly did that and then they convinced me to stay in Lima. I didn't want to let them down. I had five translation teams ready to roll. When my supervisor returned in a few months I explained my predicament and the extraordinary commitment of these young leaders, but he was furious. He said he was going to have me pulled out of the field on grounds of insubordination. I showed him how much had already been accomplished, but he didn't even want to look at any of the translation work the teams had accomplished.

"He did try to pull me from the field, but the fund raising staff in the home office liked being able to report a significant jump in translation projects underway, so my supervisor was overruled and I was able to stay in Lima. We finished all five translations and planted five churches in nine years."

"The rest of the organization must have looked at you as a hero!" said Valerie.

"No, not really. Some of the older translators were horrified and were convinced that the Bibles would be filled with errors and be substandard. Even the young translators who were working alone were opposed to this strategy. Along with them, some of our church planters didn't like having a translator planting churches. It got messy. I just tried to serve God and help these translation teams to function well."

"Then how did you get promoted?" Randall asked.

"When my supervisor retired, they didn't have anyone else available or skilled enough to serve as supervisor. This is a common problem with smaller mission organizations. So they asked me to oversee Spanish-speaking South America. I went to work visiting and encouraging our translators and church planters. I initiated annual retreats in the region. We used our new way of working for other translation projects. We soon became the smoothest functioning and most productive region in the organization.

"Later they asked me to oversee all the regions in Latin America. Some of the supervisors did not like me and they were difficult to work with. Our mission merged with another sending organization fifteen years earlier and they renamed the organization Valiant International Missions. But the staff from the two organizations never fully merged in spirit. The new president was from the other side. When I got sick and came home, the retired translators and some of the supervisors pressed for a forced retirement due to illness. The new president saw an opportunity to get rid of a potential rival. He simply sent me a letter saying I was done and channeled the funds in my account to the combined retirement fund."

"You got sick and then they threw you under the bus? How could they treat you so poorly?" asked Valerie.

"I'm not sure. That's a good question, but I have forgiven them in my heart."

"But they took your money, all the money you had raised yourself," said Randall.

"It wasn't my money, it was money given to God that happened to be in my account."

"How can a president do that and get away with it?" Brad asked.

"The organization has a policy that they can make any missionary retire due to reasons of poor health. Dedicated missionaries tend to want to stay on the mission field too long when they are sick or need rehabilitative care."

"How could they confiscate the money you had raised?" asked Brad.

"The board has a policy that any unused funds in any missionary account should be transferred to the general retirement fund."

"Why didn't you go to the board and tell them what they were doing to you?" asked Brad.

"A few of the missionaries wanted to do just that, but I told them no. I didn't think the board was strong enough to undo a decision by their new president. Besides, sometimes God allows hard things to happen because he has something else in mind for us."

"They abused you," said Lynn.

"But I'm not a victim," Jack replied as he shrugged his shoulders.

"So what are you going to do next?" asked Valerie.

"I can't do anything while on disability. So I'm simply sitting here waiting on my next assignment from the Lord. While I'm waiting, we are going to have some good conversations about leadership."

"Sounds good," said Brad. "The problems I'm facing with my board are nothing compared to what you have been through. I'm even more ready to learn everything I can from you."

Jack stood up and went to the whiteboard. "Here is your first assignment. As you go through your week, imagine how you would talk and act differently if you suddenly became the leader you were meant to be. Imagine how you would respond differently in every situation that presents itself to you. But don't actually do anything differently yet. Just observe your current behavior patterns. Ask yourself if you are talking and acting like good leader."

He wrote on the whiteboard: *Observe your behavior.*

"Why can't we change how we respond?" Randall asked.

"Because I don't want anybody getting hurt the first week of training." Then Jack grinned slightly.

4

Friday Night

Valerie wrapped the leftover slices of pizza in foil and put them in the refrigerator. Brad opened his Bible. "Let's see if we can finish Romans 13 tonight. Lynn, would you read the next paragraph for us?"

> Pay your taxes, too, for these same reasons. For government workers need to be paid. They are serving God in what they do. Give to everyone what you owe them: Pay your taxes and government fees to those who collect them, and give respect and honor to those who are in authority.

"Let's zero in on honoring those in authority over us. How does this strike you?" asked Brad.

"I do what Stan tells me to do," said Randall. "But showing honor? I don't look up to him and I probably don't show him much honor."

Valerie coughed aloud. "Excuse me, respect Tiffany? Is that what you are implying?"

"Valerie," said Lynn, "you simply need to treat her honorably. That's what I do with Dr. Hanson. When he talks to me while looking at his clipboard, which is disrespectful to me, I still treat him with respect."

"I suppose that I respect the men and women on our board, but I can't figure out what it means to give them honor. Anybody have some thoughts on that?" Brad asked.

"Do you ever honor them publicly?" asked Randall.

"No, I never mention them in my support letters either. I suppose I pretty much ignore them."

"What would it look like to give them respect and honor?" asked Lynn.

"I suppose I might start by communicating with them by email to stay in touch and let them know how things are going in our ministry. When the board chair wants to meet for coffee I probably shouldn't treat it as an interruption to my work. Funny, but I've never really thought of the board members as people before. I just saw them as positions."

"Valerie, what would happen if you viewed Tiffany as a real person? Randall, what would happen if you viewed Stan as a real person?" asked Lynn.

"That would be difficult," said Randall.

Sunday Afternoon

After leading the group back to his office, Jack came back with crackers and cubes of apples and cheese. He sat down at the table and looked at the whiteboard. "Observe your behavior. So what did you notice about your behavior?"

"I'll start out," said Brad. "I noticed that I treat the staff one way and the board members another way."

"Hmm. That's interesting," said Jack.

"While out for coffee with the board chair, I noticed I had my arms and legs crossed and I turned my body sideways away from him. It must have looked weird."

Randall raised his hand. "I saw myself waiting for Stan to tell me what to do. I was going through my shift like a guy who had his brain unplugged. I would finish a task and then go back and just stand by Stan. It's like I've been sending Stan signals to treat me this way. That's not what leaders do."

"At the clinic, I noticed that I was just accepting problems in our system, just going along with the backwards way we do things. I never got upset and I never thought about trying to change anything. I just went along with everything and tried to get along with everybody."

Valerie spoke next. "I was sitting in the lunchroom at work and I noticed that I didn't know anybody else in the room. I have worked at Synthetic Software for almost two years now and I have shied away from getting to know people from other departments. I have been cutting myself off from valuable networking relationships. If I were a leader I would be connecting more."

"Excellent," said Jack. "Next, I need to get to know each of you better. Give me a snapshot of you as a child. Tell me about your parents, especially your father."

"I suppose I watched too much television as a kid," said Valerie. "But in high school I loved to dissect full page ads in magazines and talk back to commercials. I never knew my real dad. I have a stepdad and he works a lot."

Randall said, "Both of my parents graduated from college, and they wanted their children to be successful in life, so I did a lot of homework growing up. My mother had us read books for points. My father organized fun family activities. He and I are still best friends."

"I was into sports as a kid," said Brad. "My parents divorced when I was young and my dad tried to spend a lot of time with me when I was in high school. He tried. He is a good man."

"My mom is British and my dad is Chinese. She is a nurse and he is a dentist. So I wanted to be a doctor when I grew up. My father is traditional and strict when it comes to raising children. I loved going to school."

"Thank you," said Jack. "Tell me about your current church experience. I'm interested in your level of involvement and your relationship with your pastor."

"I go to Riverview Community," said Brad. "I like the senior pastor a lot. He doesn't know me of course, but he is an excellent Bible teacher. I'm not involved at church because I'm already doing youth ministry about 55 hours a week. Suburban Life is my job and my place of volunteer service."

"I attend Sacred Heart," said Valerie. "It's near my apartment. I was raised Catholic. I suppose you could say that I'm coming back home. The priest almost knows my name, so I'm doing slightly better than Brad. I'm finding it difficult to connect with any group in the culture of this particular parish."

"I worship at New Life Assembly. Our pastor, who is the spiritual authority for our congregation, is putting pressure on me to help start a new singles ministry. I don't want to do that so I'm not volunteering at all right now."

"I'm helping out with a new multi-site launch for Faith Bible Church. I serve on the setup and tear down team. Pastor Steve is a relational leader, but he is so disorganized that it is hurting our chances of survival as a site. His decisions are causing a lot of extra work for my team each week. I'm frustrated with him."

"Now tell me about your workplace, especially your direct supervisor."

"I don't have one," said Brad. "The board of Suburban Life wants to move me into the executive director role and I'd rather just keeping working with youth. I didn't go into youth ministry to run banquets and golf outings. Last time, they hired a guy from the business world who was between jobs. I'm afraid they are going to repeat their mistake. That would be worse than continuing with no director at all."

"The corporate ladder at Synthetic Software Solutions doesn't have any rungs at the bottom. That's where I work. My supervisor is Tiffany. She is a hard-bitten marketing executive. She doesn't really acknowledge my presence unless she needs me to do something for her."

"Dr. Hanson is a recluse," said Lynn. "Nobody is allowed to knock on his door. We have to wait until he comes into the 'pit.' That's the area where all seventeen of us have our desks. Then we have to stand in line to get the information we need to do our job."

"Stan is a jerk," said Randall. "His legal first name is Stanislaw. I can't even pronounce his last name. I've been waiting two years for a promotion and got turned down for low scores on leadership. How am I supposed to demonstrate leadership when I'm under Stan's thumb all day?"

"Thank you for sharing so openly and letting me into your lives," Jack said. "I feel badly about some of the poor leadership you are currently experiencing at work. I know that you probably want advice on how you can change things at work and make it better. I can't fix your boss, but I can help you to heal."

"What? Heal?" said Brad.

Jack got up and wrote a short phrase on the whiteboard: *Follower abuse.* He looked at the four with deep compassion. "All four of you are victims of follower abuse. You have experienced so much bad leadership from your teachers, coaches, and bosses, for so many years that it has scarred you deeply. Your mental model of leadership is warped. You avoid leadership positions. You have problems relating to authority figures. You don't want anything to do with leadership."

"I had a lot of coaches who screamed at me growing up," said Brad.

"I've worked at a lot of restaurants and I've never had a good boss," said Valerie.

Lynn wiped away a tear. "It's true for me. I really don't want anything to do with being in charge. That's why I don't want to start a singles ministry."

"Follower abuse?" said Randall with a smile. "Welcome to my world. I'm living it every day at work."

"Not all follower abuse is intentional. There are four kinds of abusers and four ways to respond to follower abuse." Jack underlined the words written on the whiteboard and added four points.

Follower Abuse

- Incompetent
- Disempowering
- Manipulative
- Toxic

"Let's start with incompetent leaders. Some people mean well but they bungle their leadership role and accidentally hurt those they lead. Sometimes they are good people who are simply in the wrong position. Sometimes they are people who never bothered to work on their leadership skills. Either way, bad leadership still hurts."

"That's what Dr. Hanson is like," said Lynn. He is not a bad man. He is a doctor supervising clerical workers and bookkeepers. All of his years in med school didn't train him for that."

"Pastor Steve would also fit that category," said Randall. "He isn't trying to hurt anybody but he can't make a decision and he doesn't think ahead."

"Next is disempowering leaders," Jack continued. "Whether on purpose or by unconscious instinct, they work to cut your legs out from underneath you. They make you feel weak and dependent. So some leaders will withhold information or resources you need to do your job. Others will criticize you in front of others in a staff meeting. They make you second-guess yourself. They don't bother spending any energy affirming their followers.

"While the first two kinds of leaders may hurt you accidentally, manipulative leaders do it on purpose. They will shower you with attention or offer incentives to get you to do what they want. They will work overtime at trying to talk you into doing something. They have hidden agendas. They work behind the scenes. They want things to work out for personal benefit.

"Finally, we have toxic leaders. While manipulators take the time to be nice about it, toxic leaders don't bother. They want to hurt you. Some are screamers, some verbally criticize you and your work, some spread gossip and rumors behind your back, but they all treat you as an object instead of a human being."

"So," asked Jack, "how would you assess your current leaders?"

"Tiffany is disempowering. She always tells me that I'm on a 'need to know basis' at work. She never lets me see any sales reports before she has a chance to go over them first," said Valerie. "Last week in our staff meeting she blamed me for some ad copy that was late. I was supposed to have it done, but I'm overloaded right now because of the extra work she is piling on me."

"Nick, our former executive director was manipulative. He would ask us to change a meeting date and then never come clean with the personal reasons for rescheduling. Now that I'm thinking about it, I wonder if he manipulated the board into getting that job in the first place."

"Stan is toxic. He doesn't scream at me, but he assigns tasks harshly and only grunts if I'm doing a good job. It's like he can't bring himself to say anything positive."

"Some of the board members are toxic, too," said Brad. "They are gruff and critical in the Suburban Life board meetings. They poison the whole spirit of the board meetings."

Jack said, "No matter what kind of abuse you have repeatedly endured for years, you have a free choice. You can decide how you will respond to follower abuse." he went to the whiteboard and wrote: *Four ways to respond*. He added four points as he spoke.

Four ways to respond

- Avoid leadership roles
- Perpetuate the cycle of abuse
- Hide behind servant leadership
- Develop your unique potential

"The first way is to avoid leadership roles of any kind. You are so hurt from experiencing bad leadership that you don't want to get anywhere near it. You avoid developing yourself and let others carry the load.

"The second way to respond is to eagerly lead as you have been lead and thereby perpetuate the abuse. The bad habits of your role models are deeply engrained and you repeat their bad behaviors without knowing it.

"The third way to respond is to hide behind servant leadership. You may take on a leadership role yet avoid actually leading by claiming that you are serving your followers. Having a servant heart is important for all leaders, but that is the starting point. It's like starting blocks for sprinters. You need to start the race on your knees behind the starting line with a servant's heart, but you can't stay there. You have to run the race. Servant leaders have to actually lead.

"The fourth way to respond is by accepting the challenge to grow and develop yourself as a leader. Everybody has leadership potential. Some decide to develop themselves and grow in knowledge and skills. It is a matter of gaining clarity on how God has uniquely wired you to lead."

Jack continued, "Let's make some connections to your life. You may see yourself exhibiting several of these responses. Let's walk through them one by one."

"Nobody needs to tell me that I avoid leadership roles," said Lynn. "I've never thought about developing myself in this way before. I would never call myself a natural leader."

"Lynn, we understand that you don't view yourself as a leader, but did you notice you were the first one to speak just now?"

"But that's not leadership," said Lynn.

"You are right, it's not a position of leadership, but it is leader behavior," said Jack. "You are also concerned for the feelings of the others in the group. That is good leader behavior, too."

"I'm not avoiding leadership roles," said Randall. "I wanted that promotion. Plus, I'm assistant team leader of the setup and tear down team for church."

"At work I'm not in a position of leadership," said Valerie, "but one day I would like to be. At church I'm not leading in any way but I have started looking for a way to serve."

"Well then, you are headed the right direction," said Jack.

"Jack, I'm already leading youth and volunteers. I'm working 50 plus hours a week at it. Does not wanting to take the executive director position count as avoiding leadership roles?"

"No, you might not be a good fit for the job. Your unique potential might not match the requirements for that particular position."

"Thank you, thank you for that!" said Brad as he raised both hands in the air.

Jack pointed back to the whiteboard, "Let's look at the second way to respond, perpetuating the abuse."

After an awkward silence, Jack looked to his right. "Randall, can I ask you a question?"

"Sure," he replied.

"When you think about being promoted to a management position, would you feel pretty good about having some of the same kind of power that Stan has?"

Randall looked down at the table and then up at the ceiling. "I have to admit that it would feel pretty good. Now you've got me wondering how I would use that power. I would hope that I don't lead like Stan does."

"Who are your role models for supervising others in a work setting?"

"I don't know," said Randall. "I've never thought about that before."

Brad jumped in. "I certainly don't want to subject others to the follower abuse that I've endured. But I'm just thinking now about what kind of impact I'm having on the youth and my volunteers. I certainly never yell at them like my coaches did, but I think I am disempowering my own team by always telling them what they are doing wrong." His voice choked up but he took a deep breath and recovered quickly. "I'm just trying to help them do a better job, that's all."

"Brad, we all tend to lead the way we have been led unless we reflect deeply on our experiences, become aware of our actions, and develop our unique potential," said Jack.

"We all need to become more aware of how our actions impact others," said Lynn.

"Let's look the third way to respond, hiding behind servant leadership."

"What exactly do you mean by hiding behind servant leadership?" asked Randall.

"Well, just that. Rather than avoiding leadership roles, some people take on a role but lead poorly and then call it servant leadership. This produces follower abuse."

"So if it is a good thing to be a servant, and you work hard to do it well, how does that make you a bad leader who is causing follower abuse?" Lynn asked. "I think the more servanthood we have the better."

"Those who hide behind servant leadership are not serving well, Lynn. They are passive leaders who excuse their lack of action as servant leadership. They may have a servant's heart but they are confusing ineffective, passive leadership behavior with genuine servant leadership which is highly active.

Randall leaned toward Lynn. "I can see what you are saying, but this is exactly what Pastor Steve does. In our first team meeting last year, he came in and asked how we wanted the team to run. We said we didn't know and why didn't he just tell us what the goals were for our team, how we fit into the larger picture, and how we should go about setup and tear down. He smiled and said, 'Oh no, I would never think of telling you what to do. I'm a servant leader.' He was afraid to give us the direction we needed and were asking for. He couldn't make a simple decision and that held us all back."

"In other words," said Valerie, "the more servant heart we have the better, but we need to make sure we are still taking care of people and getting something done."

"Jack, we are all graduates of Divine Servant University," said Brad. "You have to understand that we have had servant leadership drilled into us for four years, so this idea is difficult for us to grasp."

"Sounds like you had the concept of active leadership drilled out of you at the same time."

"They taught us to never, ever put ourselves above others," said Lynn.

"And that's Biblical," said Jack. "Hold on to that teaching tightly. But humble people can take decisive actions. Those with servant hearts can be action-oriented servants."

Brad sat up straighter in his chair. "That just pushed one of my buttons. I'm feeling eager to grow as a leader."

"Let's move to the fourth way to respond, developing your unique potential. Where are you all at on this one?" Jack asked.

"I would like to think that I've been developing my unique potential," said Valerie, "but I have never read a leadership book that wasn't assigned reading for a class. I've never had a mentor. I've never consciously tried to improve my leadership."

"I've read a couple leadership books over the years," said Brad. "I find those written about ministry leadership more helpful than secular books."

"I still don't want to be the boss," said Lynn. "But if I focus on developing my unique potential, I think that would be doable. That means just becoming who I am more fully. I want to do that."

"I've studied great leaders in history," said Randall, "so I suppose that counts. But I haven't really done anything to put those leadership insights into practice."

"Well I think you all have a handle on the four ways to respond.

I just wish more people would determine to develop their unique potential," said Jack. Everybody has leadership potential. Some work on discovering it and developing themselves. Others let their potential lay dormant. I have no idea what kind of leadership potential is deep within each of you. But if you want my help, then you have to be totally committed to meeting together, following through, and reporting back."

"We're ready now," said Brad. "When do we start learning how to lead?"

"Not yet. Your mental model of leadership is warped. Your first assignment is to make a list of all the significant leaders in your life from your parents to your current supervisor. Include coaches, teachers, and other influential people. List any follower abuse you experienced under their leadership and how this has impacted your view of leadership. Then list how they modeled good leadership to you and the positive effect these had on your view of leadership. Come back next week prepared to tell me what good leadership looks like."

"This feels like the kind of exercise you would find in a self-help book," said Randall.

"All leader development is ultimately self-development," said Jack.

5

Friday Night

Brad sat on the floor and opened his Bible to Genesis. "Hey guys, listen to what I discovered this week while doing my devotions. Joseph was a victim of follower abuse. You know the story. First he suffered verbal and physical abuse from his older brothers. By selling him into slavery, he became a victim of human trafficking. Then he faced attempted sexual abuse from Potiphar's wife. Then Potiphar threw him in prison even though he was serving him so well. Then Pharoah's chief cup-bearer left him behind in prison."

"Joseph was crushed again and again," said Valerie. "He must have been deeply scarred by all of that."

"That's probably the worst story of follower abuse in the Bible," said Randall.

"But Joseph didn't give up or give in. Here is what he tells his brothers in Genesis 50:20."

> *You intended to harm me, but God intended it all for good. He brought me to this position so I could save the lives of many people.*

Randall sat up a little straighter. "There was a purpose behind it all."

"God worked it all together for good," said Lynn.

"Yes," Valerie added, "but it took a lot of bad years before he saw his first good one."

"This puts a new slant on our assignment." Brad slid his bookmark in his Bible and closed it. "So what were some, shall we say, highlights from your list of bad leaders?"

Randall leaned forward. "I worked on a house painting crew one summer. My boss, who was only two years older than me, kept telling me what I was doing wrong and pointing out my errors. It killed my motivation. I checked out mentally. I couldn't wait for college to start in the fall."

"I used to work in a Christian bookstore on Saturdays," said Lynn. "The manager was only interested in books, not people, and certainly not employees. The only training he gave me for the job was how to work the cash register. I was on my own learning how to serve customers. Sometimes they would ask about a special order. If I didn't know the procedure, the manager would swoop in and take care of it. I felt like a stupid assistant in front of the customer. It eroded my sense of confidence in dealing with people."

"I waitressed for five summers at different restaurants, whoever happened to be hiring," said Valerie. "Customers often treated me like a position. The owner never bothered to learn my name. The manager sat behind the cash register all morning and never talked to any of us. I felt ignored and insignificant. I started becoming more passive at work and less concerned about the customers."

"I had a basketball coach for two years who yelled excessively at the players during practices and games. We worked hard out of fear and embarrassment, but it also impacted me by making me less of a team player. I was focusing on avoiding mistakes instead of making great plays," Brad said.

Then he asked, "Did God intend these experiences for good in our lives?"

"I'm not seeing it yet," said Valerie.

"I can see some good coming through it," said Randall. "Stan is giving me a crash course on how not to lead."

Sunday Afternoon

Jack welcomed everyone to his office. He had whole pieces of fruit in a bowl for them with knives and small wooden platters for cutting the fruit. Jack asked about what they learned from the assignment and they all shared their new insights.

"You were right about the impact of bad leadership on our lives," said Valerie. "So now we are all hooked on developing our unique potential, each for different reasons. Brad wants to do better ministry, Randall wants to qualify for a promotion, Lynn wants to learn how to deal with manipulative people, and I want to do more with my life and grow."

"When we first came to you we were not interested in leadership development, we just wanted some life coaching," said Brad. "Now that we see what developing our unique potential can do for us, we are ready to grow as leaders."

"Yes, we get it now," Lynn said.

"Okay," said Jack, "so you are telling me that you are ready to grow. You all have gotten to this point faster than I anticipated."

"We are surprising you?" asked Randall.

"Uh, let's say I'm pleasantly surprised. It's rare. Many people don't make it this far you know," said Jack.

"Wow, I've never thought about that before," said Brad.

Jack sat back in his chair and pressed his fingertips together. Remaining perfectly still he took a few moments to look each of them in the eye. Then he smiled softly. "We are going to skip reporting out on last week's assignment. We are going to skip a few other preliminary assignments as well. I think you are ready to get at the heart of leadership."

"I'm ready," said Valerie.

"Let's turn to Psalm 78:72. This part of the Psalm is about how God called David into leadership and took him from shepherding animals to shepherding the people of Israel. Follow along with me as I read. In fact, put your finger under each word as I read this passage." Jack read the verse three times.

> *He cared for them with a true heart and led them*
> *with skillful hands.*

"What do you observe in this passage?" asked Jack.

Brad spoke first. "Well, the 'he' refers to David."

"He cared for the people he led," said Lynn.

Brad said, "He led the people skillfully."

"This verse is about a leader and what he was like on the inside and outside," said Randall.

"Right," said Jack. "There is a being side and a doing side to leadership. You cannot neglect either one. You need both character and competence to lead well. Books by business leaders tend to neglect the being side. They usually jump right into leader actions. Books by church leaders tend to neglect the doing side. They focus almost exclusively on character and spiritual formation issues. You need to grow in both just as David did. Don't let go of either one."

"So," Brad said, "which side of leadership are we going to start with?"

"Neither. David is an example of the kind of leaders we want to become. Envision yourself having developed both a true heart and skillful hands to lead. This represents our destination," said Jack.

"So what is our next step?" asked Brad.

"If you want to learn how to lead, you must first learn to follow well," said Jack.

After a long silence, Randall spoke softly to no one in particular, "That's counter-intuitive."

"Jack, I don't get it. Can you help me connect the dots here?" asked Brad.

"When you are a leader, you lead followers," said Jack. "If you know how to follow well, then you know what good followers need. If you don't know how to follow well yourself, you won't be able to help others follow well."

"But following is easy," said Brad.

"Perhaps, but I'm talking about following well. We are going to focus on following well for the next few weeks. We can't go any further if you don't master this," said Jack.

"A few weeks? Are you kidding?" asked Valerie.

"I want you to start keeping a leadership development journal. You need to make an entry every day. It can be a reflection on something that happened or just something you are thinking about. It needs to cover both the being side and the doing side every day," said Jack.

"We can do that," said Randall.

"Let's take a good hard look at what it means to follow well," Jack said. "When I was supervising Bible translators and church planters, I scheduled a retreat for the missionaries in my region every year. In one of those retreats we focused on followership. We took a whole day to write down every verse about following well that we could find in the Bible. Then we took the next day to organize these passages into a few main categories that would help us define what it means to follow well. We had what you might call an 'energetic' discussion that second day. We taped the verses to a wall and spent hours moving them around in various configurations."

Jack got up from his chair and opened his desk drawer. He reached towards the back and pulled out a stack of old three-by-five cards taller than he could grasp with one hand. He placed them on the center of the table with a thump. They were smudged with sweaty fingerprints. "We had a couple categorization schemes that worked, but the clear winner was the one we named R.E.A.L. The letters stand for responsible, ethical, authentic, and loving. We landed on this one because it was shorter than some of our other solutions that had seven or eight categories. Plus, it spelled an actual word. We also liked that it works in both English and Spanish."

"Of course!" said Valerie.

"So a REAL follower is responsible, ethical, authentic, and loving. It sounds easy enough," said Lynn.

Jack frowned slightly and looked down at the table but said nothing. He went to the whiteboard and drew a chart with the four key words down the side and the phrase *following well* at the top.

Following Well	
Responsible	
Ethical	
Authentic	
Loving	

"Let's take one cell at a time. Describe the heart of a follower who is responsible," said Jack. He pulled the lid off the marker to capture their thoughts on the whiteboard.

"Well," Brad said, "it would be a person who does not shirk his or her duties. This person is not a slacker."

"He or she is self-disciplined," said Randall.

"This would be someone willing to be accountable," said Valerie.

"They would want all of their work to be quality," said Lynn.

"They complete their assignments and finish their work," said Randall.

Valerie added, "They help out without being asked."

Jack nodded, "Let's explore what the Bible has to say about being a responsible follower."

Jack took the laptop off of his desk and opened the lid. He launched a Bible search program. "Now we are going to see if your expensive education at Divine Servant had any lasting effects. Work together to find three passages about being a responsible follower. You can use your phone, this laptop, a Bible, or your sanctified memory banks."

They got to work. Randall reached for the computer and quickly typed a word. Jack waited a few seconds and then said, "I'll give you a hint. If you type in the word 'responsible' you are going to come up dry. That's the category name. Search for key words related to the meaning we just brainstormed."

"Try 'self-discipline,' Randall," Brad said.

"Here we go. 1 Thessalonians 5:6." Randall read it to them.

> *So be on your guard, not asleep like the others. Stay alert and be clearheaded.*

"Good," said Jack. "How about some of these other aspects of being responsible?"

"Here's one that might work," said Valerie. "Ephesians 6:7."

> *Work with enthusiasm, as though you were working*
> *for the Lord rather than for people.*

"I have one," said Lynn. "I Corinthians 4:2."

> *Now, a person who is put in charge as a manager must*
> *be faithful.*

"Hey, my new life verse!" said Randall.

"Isn't that more of a leadership verse?" asked Brad.

"True, but the manager has to follow his boss. Plus it would apply to any follower put in charge of something," said Jack.

"I can agree with that," said Brad.

"Let's move to the next row. What does it mean for a follower to be an ethical person?" asked Jack.

"An ethical person will be concerned for justice and want others to be treated fairly," said Valerie.

"Ethical followers do what is right. They follow the rules. They avoid cheating, stealing, and stretching the truth," said Brad.

"They never manipulate people," said Lynn.

"Good," said Jack, "easy to explain but hard to do. What are some passages that come to mind?"

"I already typed in the word 'ethical' and it came up blank," said Randall.

"Oh, here's a good one, 1 Corinthians 10:24." Valerie read it aloud.

> *Don't be concerned for your own good but for the good*
> *of others.*

"Here's another one, 1 Peter 2:15," said Lynn.

*It is God's will that your honorable lives should silence
those ignorant people who make foolish accusations
against you.*

Brad said, "Jackpot. Here's a whole Psalm that touches on being an
ethical follower, Psalm 15. I'll just read verses 1-4."

*Who may worship in your sanctuary, Lord? Who
may enter your presence on your holy hill? Those who
lead blameless lives and do what is right, speaking the
truth from sincere hearts. Those who refuse to gossip
or harm their neighbors or speak evil of their friends.
Those who despise flagrant sinners, and honor the
faithful followers of the Lord, and keep their promises
even when it hurts.*

"Good," said Jack. "Now tell me what an authentic follower is like."

"Authentic followers are being themselves at all times," Valerie said.
"They are genuine and humble."

"They are not prideful," said Lynn.

"In terms of doing, they treat people respectfully, they are self-
disclosing, they are straight shooters," said Brad.

"FYI, I typed in the word 'authentic' and it came up blank again.
Switch over to memory cells." said Randall.

"Romans 12:3 will work," said Brad.

*Because of the privilege and authority God has given
me, I give each of you this warning: Don't think
you are better than you really are. Be honest in your
evaluation of yourselves, measuring yourselves by the
faith God has given us.*

"Philippians 2:3 might help us," said Lynn.

> *Don't be selfish; don't try to impress others. Be humble, thinking of others as better than yourselves.*

"Psalm 51:17 is a good one," said Valerie.

> *The sacrifice you desire is a broken spirit. You will not reject a broken and repentant heart, O God.*

"That takes us to the last one, which is easy to understand and difficult to actually do: loving," said Jack.

"A person with love in his or her heart is usually a kind individual," said Lynn.

"A loving person has a heart overflowing with love," said Valerie, "and he or she does not look down on others."

"They don't hold grudges," said Randall.

"They treat people as they would like to be treated," said Valerie.

"I think I've got all the verses we need for this one," said Randall. "Let's start out with 1 Corinthians 13:4."

> *Love is patient and kind. Love is not jealous or boastful or proud.*

"1 Corinthians 13 is a classic passage on love," said Valerie.

"1 Peter 4:8 is looking promising," said Randall.

> *Most important of all, continue to show deep love for each other, for love covers a multitude of sins.*

"And we can wrap it up with Colossians 3:14," he added.

Above all, clothe yourselves with love, which binds us
all together in perfect harmony.

Jack captured the verse references on the whiteboard and then sat down at the table. "Does it make sense that following well requires all four of these attributes? You can't follow well if you are irresponsible. You can't follow well if you are acting unethically in any way. You can't follow well if you are faking it or lording it over others, in other words not being your true humble self. If you follow extraordinarily well but didn't love others, you would have gained nothing."

"No argument there, Jack, but this is all rather basic," said Brad.

"I think we can all see the importance of these biblical principles of Christian living," Valerie said. "All believers are supposed to be doing this anyway."

"Good," said Jack, "that is exactly right. So here is your next assignment. Simply try to follow well this week in every role where you are following a leader."

"Okay," said Randall.

"Sure," said Valerie.

Jack leaned slightly forward and looked in the eyes of each of them. "Let me clarify the assignment. You are going to be a REAL follower at work and at church. That means you are going to be responsible, ethical, authentic, and loving."

"It can't be that hard," said Lynn.

"Okay, pop quiz," said Jack. "Raise your hand to indicate your answer. How many of you love your boss?" No one raised their hand.

"How many of you pray for your boss?" Still no hands were raised.

"Uh oh, not Stan," said Randall.

"Yes, especially Stan," said Jack.

"Jack, do you realize what you are asking of me? He is a toxic leader.

He calls me 'dipstick' all the time."

"Hold on a minute. Why does he call you dipstick?" asked Brad.

"Well, my first week on the job I didn't know what to do so he told me to check the oil on the forklift. I was looking all over the machine for about five or six minutes. Stan was sending some of the other guys to the loading dock to look at me checking the oil. Then he walked over and held up the plug. It was an electric fork lift. So he started calling me dipstick after that."

Jack laughed. "It doesn't matter what he calls you. You can still be a follower who treats him in a loving way."

"How can I do that?" asked Randall.

"If you are genuinely looking for some guidance, you can start by learning how to pronounce his name," said Jack.

"I'm not sure how to complete the assignment in my situation," said Brad. "I'm really not following an individual leader at church or work."

"Well let's start with your board. What would it mean to be a REAL follower of the board?" asked Jack.

"Well, I would have to be more enthusiastic about meeting with them. I would give them more reports on what is happening in the ministry. But wait, that's just what they want from me! Then I would be acting like the Executive Director. I don't want to be a REAL follower of the board. Boards don't count for this assignment, do they?" asked Brad.

"Each and every board member counts," said Jack.

Jack looked at the two girls. "What will this mean for you two?"

"For me it would mean having to change my attitude toward Tiffany," said Valerie. "I can work on that. But it won't be easy."

"I don't think this will be difficult to do with Dr. Hanson. But I don't want to even try being a REAL follower with Pastor Howard. I don't want to launch a new ministry," said Lynn.

"Following well does not mean doing everything he asks or tells you to do. That would be mindless obedience. It does, however, mean being authentic and genuine with him. If you start avoiding him you cannot call that following well," said Jack.

"I'll keep thinking about what I can do differently," said Lynn.

"The assignment once again is to follow well, at work and at church, in every role where you are following somebody. Make a journal entry each day about what you are learning about following well," said Jack.

"Sounds like this is going to be a 'real' week," Randall said as he made air quotes with his fingers.

6

Monday Afternoon

Brad slowly picked up his cell phone and scrolled to a name and tapped the talk button. "Steve, this is Brad, how are you today?"

"Good, Brad, what's up?" asked Steve.

"I have a favor to ask. When we go to Riverview this weekend would you help me stay awake for the teaching?" asked Brad.

"Sure, dude, why the sudden burst of self-discipline?"

"I'm just trying to be more responsible in different areas of life. I don't actually have to take on more responsibility at church, but it is a bit irresponsible for me to be sleeping during the sermon."

"Okay, glad to do it. I'll meet you inside as usual."

Brad slid his phone in his pocket and walked to the meeting room for the staff meeting. Bob, Joe, Beth, and Mary were already in the room. Bob and Mary were flicking a folded sheet of paper toward each other in a game of tabletop football. Joe was answering a text message, and Beth was checking voicemail.

Brad took a seat at the table. "Before we move to our regular agenda, I wanted to ask you guys about how we ought to relate to the board of directors during this time when we have no executive director."

"What's there to discuss?" asked Bob.

"Well, I'm just trying to be a more responsible follower. I thought that we should all communicate with them more. I thought we could keep them updated on how the ministry is going. Maybe we could attend the board meetings sending one or two of us each time."

"I don't get it," said Bob. "Why should any of us go to any board meetings?"

"This would give us a chance to get to know them and they could get to know us," said Brad.

"What's the point of getting to know them?" asked Mary.

"They are our board. It's important. They are volunteering their time to our organization, and they have needs too." said Brad.

"Well you can count me out," said Bob. "I'm not wasting any of my free time going to a board meeting."

"I don't want to get to know any of the board members," said Beth.

"Sounds like there's no need to take a vote. Scratch my suggestion. We'll stick with the standard written ministry reports for the board," said Brad. "Who's going to lead the staff meeting today?"

Lynn walked over to the desk of a co-worker in the 'pit.' "Marie, I was looking at the stack of unprocessed paperwork on my desk. Everybody has stacks like this. Most of the time we are waiting for input or a sign-off from a nurse, and they put this off until the end of each day. We are spending a lot of time waiting for them to get back to us. It seems like there has to be a better way of handling these forms."

"There probably is," said Marie, then she calmly went back to her paperwork.

"Don't you think we should try to do something about this?"

"Nope, not my job," said Marie without looking up.

In the lunch room Lynn sat down by four other women and asked them about the idea of meeting together to try to improve the existing procedures. "Would any of you go with me to talk to the nurses about this issue?"

One of the older women spoke for the group, "Lynn, honey, if you don't shut up about our procedures people are going to start wondering who died and made you queen of the office. Don't you think we know there are problems? Don't you think we would have fixed them already if they were fixable? Dr. Hanson is the problem here, not us. And Dr. Hanson is the supervisor here, not you."

VALERIE STOPPED BY TIFFANY'S OFFICE and knocked on the open door. "Excuse me, Tiffany."

"Hi," Tiffany responded without smiling.

"I'm going to the lunchroom to get some fresh coffee. Would you like me to get you a refill?"

Tiffany narrowed her eyes. "What are you up to?"

"I just thought that you might appreciate some more coffee."

"Sure." She handed Valerie her cup. "Be sure to empty out the old coffee first."

An hour later, Valerie and Tiffany were in the same informational meeting. A vice president asked for some assistance with a cross-departmental project. Valerie volunteered to help. After the meeting, Tiffany called her into her office.

"What do you think you are doing?"

"What do you mean?"

"Why did you volunteer for that hair-brained project?"

"I was just trying to be a responsible employee. Another department needed some help and I thought it was the right thing to do."

"Don't ever volunteer for an assignment without checking with me first. We can't afford to be utilizing our limited resources on unbudgeted projects. Let me remind you that your title is Marketing Associate. That means that you work in the marketing department, got it?"

"What about the current project?"

"It's too late to undo that decision now after you made it so public. Just try to get it done and get back to your own work as soon as possible."

RANDALL WALKED BACK TO THE LOADING dock and noticed two pallets of vegetables that were awkwardly left in the walkway. He looked around and saw that nobody was caring for them. So he walked to the forklift, put on the hardhat, jumped into the seat, and drove it to pallets. He expertly moved them out of the walkway and near a wall. When he returned the forklift, he saw Stan waiting for him.

"Hey, dipstick, did I tell you to move those pallets?"

"No," said Randall, "I just thought it might be good..."

Stan tapped his pencil on the side of his hardhat. "So, you were thinking, were you? We'll I'll give you something to think about. I do the thinking around here and you do the doing. I want you to spend some time thinking about that. Any questions?"

"Well, I was just trying to be responsible. The pallets seemed like they were in an inconvenient place so I thought I would move them to where they are supposed to be."

"They are supposed to be where I want them to be and no place else. How would you like it if I came to your house and moved your furniture around?"

"Stan, I'm sorry."

"The floor out here is looking dirty. Grab a broom and sweep up this whole area."

"I'm on it!"

LYNN SAT IN PASTOR SMITH'S OFFICE. She explained her reluctance about leading the new ministry for young adults.

"Lynn, as you well know, the church functions differently than the world. We operate by spiritual authority. Authority is a good thing. When you signed the covenant for membership you were placing yourself under the spiritual authority of this congregation. As the leader, I'm simply telling you what we feel is God's will for you. I'd hate for you to be willfully disobedient. I'm concerned for your spiritual health and growth most of all. It would be good for you to be involved in this kind of ministry."

"But Pastor Howard, I don't want to do it. I don't think I would be good at it."

"Lynn, by the spiritual authority vested in me as pastor of this church, I'm saying that we all want you to do this. Yes?"

"Okay," said Lynn. "I'll try to launch this new ministry."

"Splendid. I would recommend forming a committee to help you plan a big launch," he said.

Friday Night

Brad sat on the floor of Valerie's apartment with his Bible on the floor next to him. "Let's just check in with each other first. How is it going for you trying to follow well in all areas of life?"

"I tried being a REAL follower and it is only making things worse!" said Randall. "Stan chewed me out for moving some pallets. I was just trying to be responsible. I told him I was sorry, and that didn't do much either."

"It's making things worse for me, too," said Valerie. "I stepped up and volunteered for a special project, and Tiffany jumped all over me. Now I'm on a much shorter leash. I can't volunteer for anything without checking with her first. I had more freedom when I was less responsible."

"I tried to organize a meeting to talk about our work procedures and I hit a wall. The older women don't want to talk about their work and they certainly don't want me to call the meeting. Trying to follow well at work is scary. All the other employees have been there longer than me. I'm the youngest one there. It's like they don't want me to follow well."

"That's an interesting point, Lynn," said Brad. "I wanted to try to follow well with the board, but the rest of the staff just didn't get it. I gave up after the first try. I couldn't follow well with the board because of my co-workers."

"It seems that we are all getting resistance to our attempts to follow well," said Randall.

Lynn started to cry. "I have to buy a new car and my dad is telling me what kind to buy. I will be paying for it myself, and I don't want a Honda Civic."

"Well, why don't you just tell your dad that you want something else?" asked Brad.

"You don't know my dad. He simply expects me to obey. I met with Pastor Howard too. He told me I was under the spiritual authority of the congregation and that I needed to do the ministry they were asking me to do."

"Why didn't you just say no?" asked Randall.

"Because I agreed to put myself under the spiritual authority of the congregation," said Lynn.

"But not the pastor," said Randall.

"He is the spiritual leader of the congregation. The Bible says we are to obey those in authority," Lynn began to cry again, "and I was just trying to follow well." Valerie put her arm around her.

"Let's say we took the Bible seriously and obeyed those in authority above us. That would mean I would have to do what the board said and take the executive director position. I am in their employment, after all. Lynn would get stuck with a used Civic. What about the rest of you?""

"I can't just do everything Tiffany asks. She is a manipulator. She does not have my best interests in mind. I have to protect myself by setting clear boundaries with her," said Valerie.

"I do everything Stan tells me, so in one sense I'm submitting to his authority, at least on the outside. On the inside I can't follow him. He is my boss, sure, but he is not my leader. I don't respect him enough for that. Following him well seems unattainable," said Randall.

"Do you think Jack will be upset with us because we have not followed well this week?" asked Lynn.

"I think he will be pleased that we all made an attempt this week," said Valerie.

"I think he is assuming we made an attempt this week, otherwise we won't be allowed to meet with him anymore," said Randall.

"I suspect that Jack knew we would all hit resistance," Brad said.

Sunday Afternoon

Betty welcomed the four leaders-in-training and brought them back to Jack's office. "Jack made some special Peruvian trail mix for you all. It's one of his favorites."

"Yeah, a special trail mix for those on a journey in life," Jack said.

Jack asked for a briefing on the week. Each told how they tried to follow well and the reactions they received from others. Jack listened intently without giving advice.

Before Jack could set the agenda for the day, Brad spoke up. "Jack, we have got to talk about the problems we are having with following those in authority over us. Following well is only making it worse for us. What about Lynn's pastor? Should Valerie submit to her supervisor?"

"And what about my situation?" Randall asked. "Should I stop thinking at work like Stan told me? If I obey him, like I'm supposed to, then I am automatically not following well. I'm in a catch-22."

"You all are," Jack said. He sat silently smiling at each of them in turn.

"Good questions. Good work this week. I'm proud of all of you. Let's clear up the confusion in your thinking regarding following those in authority." Jack got up and went to the blank whiteboard. He reached up higher than normal and drew three tall columns. He titled the columns: *Type I, Type II, Type III.*

"We'd better buckle our seat belts for this one," Randall said.

"There are three different types of followership. Type I is 'following God.' Type II is 'following inherited authorities.' You're probably wondering what that means. Type III is 'following human beings.'" He wrote those phrases across the first row.

"Type I is following God. This is the most demanding of the three types of followership. We are to love God with all our heart, all our soul, all our strength, and all our mind. That pretty much means giving it everything we've got. As followers of Jesus, we are commanded to love others, we are commanded to make disciples, and we are commanded to love each other. Those are commands, not helpful hints for a more fulfilling life.

"Open your Bibles to Matthew 16:24. What does it say?" Randall read it for the group.

> *Then Jesus said to his disciples, "If any of you wants to be my follower, you must turn from your selfish ways, take up your cross, and follow me."*

"Type I followership means denying yourself, enduring suffering, and being willing to die as you follow Jesus, your leader.

"Type II followership is a lot easier in comparison. Inherited authorities include your parents and the government. When you were born into this world you were born into a family or adopted by one. Your parents had authority over you. You were also born into a nation with laws and rulers. They have civil authority over you. You had no choice in these matters. You inherited them when you were born. As a child, you are to honor and obey your parents. You had rules in your house you had to follow. As an adult, you are to give honor to governmental officials and obey the laws of the land. The Bible is exceedingly clear on this.

"Turn to Romans 13 and read the first verse." Valerie read it aloud.

> *Everyone must submit to governing authorities. For all authority comes from God, and those in positions of authority have been placed there by God.*

"This passage is talking about government. It includes elected officials, appointed officials, federal, state, and local governments. It includes police, military, and tax-collecting functions. God wants us to submit to their authority, which by the way, comes from God.

"Note carefully that it does not include businesses, nonprofit organizations, ministries, churches, denominations, or other nongovernmental organizations. Those fall into the last type of followership.

"Type III involves following another human being. You are free to follow any leader or free not to follow. The choice is yours. Another person may use rewards or threats to try to make you do what they want, but all they get is mere compliance instead of true followership.

"Within Type III, there are low authority settings and high authority settings. Let's say an advocate for an environmental cause is speaking in a public gathering. The leader will try to persuade and motivate, but the choice of whether or not to follow is up to the listeners. The leader has no organizational authority to make them comply and join the cause. Those who follow well tend to choose good leaders to follow.

"Organizational authority adds another variable. A CEO of a large manufacturing corporation may have authority to shut down entire divisions or purchase other companies. A foreman may have the authority to hire and fire assembly line workers. If your boss has authority over you, you are free to follow him or her or not follow. If your boss wants you to do something you don't want to do, you can quit and work for a different boss. You may face financial consequences, but the choice is still up to you.

"Type III followership is socially constructed and entirely negotiable. If you don't like the way your manager is treating you, then you can talk to him or her about it. If you want to add a new area of responsibility, you can ask for it. It doesn't matter if you are a paid employee or a volunteer. It's just that volunteer organizations will tend to be more responsive.

"But we easily confuse the organizational authority of Type III followership with the governmental authority of Type II followership.

We don't have to submit to our bosses at work in the same way. Rather, we should simply attempt to follow well.

"Let's turn to Matthew 7:12. Read it for me please."

> *Do to others whatever you would like them to do to you. This is the essence of all that is taught in the law and the prophets.*

"In Type III followership, you follow a boss, supervisor, manager, or leader who is a human being and created in the image of God. That means every verse in Scripture that tells us how to treat other people applies to your relationship with your leader. But this is easy to forget on the job.

"In Type I, we are unable to follow God apart from the work of the Holy Spirit in our hearts. In Type II, we are forced to follow. In Type III, we are free to follow. Obedience is mandatory in Type II and voluntary in Type III.

"In Type I, follower abuse is impossible. God loves us and will care for us forever. In Type II, follower abuse is common. Power corrupts. That's why most governments have checks and balances and ways to hold officials accountable. In Type III, follower abuse happens. But we don't have to put up with it."

"In Type I followership is eternal, in Type II it is lifetime, and in Type III it is always temporary."

Jack filled in the last row of the chart.

Type I	Type II		Type III	
Following God	Following Inherited Authorities		Following Human Beings	
Spiritual authority	Parental authority	Legal authority	With authority	Without authority
Unable to follow	Forced to follow		Free to follow	
Abuse is impossible	Abuse is common		Abuse happens	
Eternal	Lifetime		Temporary	

Randall raised his hand. "That's a clear explanation. Type I is following God, Type II is following an inherited authority, and Type III is following another human being. But what if there is a conflict between them. For example, what if you are trying to follow well at work and the supervisor asks you to do something illegal?"

"Good question. If you are striving to follow well that doesn't happen very often. But the rule of thumb when there is a conflict is that Type II followership always trumps Type III. And if the government or your boss intrudes in matters of faith, Type I followership trumps both of the others."

"But what about Lynn's pastor?" asked Valerie.

"What kind of followership problem is this? What do you all think?" asked Jack.

"Well it's either Type I or Type III," said Randall.

"This is Type III. This not about Lynn's connection to Jesus, it's about following another human being who happens to be a pastor," said Brad.

"It's about volunteering in an organization that happens to be a local church," said Valerie.

"So what should Lynn do?" asked Jack.

"Well," said Randall, "I suppose that she is free to follow or not to follow. So that means she can say yes or no to the pastor."

"That means she can change her mind," said Valerie with a smile.

"But what if the pastor gets upset with me?" asked Lynn.

"He is a human being. You should deal with it as you would with any human being who is upset with you," said Brad. "You should talk about it with him and try to live in harmony with all people as much as possible."

"But he keeps telling me that according to the Bible he is in spiritual authority over me," said Lynn.

"Let's take a closer look at the way spiritual authority works in Type I followership," said Jack. "Spiritual leadership functions differently than human leadership. In Type I, all people are following God. Jesus is the leader and we are the followers. We will always remain followers of God for eternity. A leader in Type I is someone who comes alongside people and helps them become connected to Jesus. A leader stays alongside and helps them grow spiritually and become more like Jesus. A spiritual leader never inserts himself or herself between Jesus and the believer. He or she is a guide alongside.

"Pastors of local churches have two kinds of authority. When they preach and teach the Bible to us we must follow with a Type I followership. Their preaching and teaching ought to make us better followers of Jesus. When they lead and make decisions regarding buildings and programs and staffing, we should follow with a Type III followership. At that point we are following another human being with some degree of organizational authority. We should follow well, but many of the details are negotiable."

Jack turned to speak directly to Lynn. "Your pastor is confusing the two kinds of authority, but you can keep them distinct as you strive to follow well at church."

"But what about Hebrews 13:17? He often mentions this passage when he wants people to submit to his authority."

"Let's take a close look at that passage," said Jack.

Randall quickly pulled it up on his phone. "Here it is."

> *Obey your spiritual leaders, and do what they say. Their work is to watch over your souls, and they are accountable to God. Give them reason to do this with joy and not with sorrow. That would certainly not be for your benefit.*

"Let's think carefully about this verse. Doesn't it sound like the author of Hebrews was simply telling believers to follow well? Perhaps many back then were not following well and they were causing their leaders much sorrow. We should avoid that. We should follow our leaders well so they can lead us with joy and gratitude. When they teach us God's truth we need to follow with a Type I followership. When they are leading people we need to follow well with a Type III followership. You are under no obligation to submit to everything a pastor might tell you to do."

"That makes me feel relieved," said Lynn.

"This is going to help me at church, too," said Randall.

"Your assignment this week is to follow well, this time distinguishing between the three types of followership and acting accordingly. In every role, ask yourself what it would mean for me to follow well."

7

Wednesday Morning

Lynn waited until the church office opened at 9:00 a.m. and then she called. "Hi, I'd like to leave a voicemail message for Pastor Howard please."

"You can do that but today is his day off and he can't get back to you until tomorrow afternoon," said the secretary.

"I was aware this was his day off, thank you." The secretary connected her and the voicemail message said to begin speaking at the sound of the beep. "Hi Pastor, this is Lynn Chiang. I changed my mind and decided not to help lead the new ministry to younger adults. I just don't think it's a good match for me. Thank you for serving as our pastor. I appreciate your solid Bible teaching every week. Please give me a call should you have any questions." Lynn pushed the button to end the call and exhaled deeply.

RANDALL WAS STOCKING CANS OF VEGETABLES in the produce department for a special display. Stan walked by and then stopped and turned around. He noticed Randall inspecting each can as he stacked them.

"Let me show you a faster way to do that, kid. Cut the box on the back side like this, lift it up to the display, then cut the other two sides and pull it back. Whole box, one motion."

"Stan, I can't do that. Some of these cans are dented."

"We always sell cans that are dented. A little dent doesn't matter."

"Stan, if one of these old-style cans is dented on a seam we have to take it off the shelf. It's a health regulation."

"Just do it my way and get it done, dipstick."

"Stan, no. If I did this I could get us both into trouble. What if the health department inspects this display? I know it's unlikely, but why risk a reprimand for you and a citation for the store?"

Stan stood in front of him with his fists on his hips and eyes glaring. "Fine." Then he turned and walked away.

Brad was the first in the room for the weekly staff meeting. Bob, Joe, Mary, and Beth arrived within minutes. "As we start our meeting today, I wanted to run something by you guys. I'm trying to figure out what it means to follow well when you attend a mega-church and work in ministry more than full-time like we do. Should I be trying to get more involved at Riverview?"

"That would be a good thing. I help out with a couple annual events at my church and it helps me connect with the body of believers there," said Mary.

"I'm not so sure," said Beth. "Ministry leaders need to be concerned for their own soul care. It's easy to get burned out. But getting involved in another ministry when you are already in ministry full-time doesn't sound like the right solution for you."

Joe pointed his pen toward Brad. "You know the church policy for Suburban Life. Every staff person has to attend worship regularly. You don't have to join. You don't have to get involved. If you want to get technical, it doesn't even have to be the same church every week. I think you are currently fulfilling organizational requirements. You don't have to do anything extra."

"Yeah, but that assumes I'm awake for the entire sermon," said Brad.

"Or just keep falling asleep as usual and download the podcast each week to catch what you missed when you work out," said Bob.

"Brad, Riverview doesn't need you. They have all the volunteers they need for their programs and ministries," said Beth.

"Thanks," said Brad, "It's just that sitting through a one-hour service once a week doesn't seem like following well at church. I don't know what I should be doing."

VALERIE STOPPED BY TIFFANY'S OFFICE and knocked on the open door. "Hi Tiffany, I've got a question for you."

"Well then make it quick, I'm waiting for a phone call."

"I got your email to merge the new email list with our current subscribers. I was able to track down the spreadsheet with the new email addresses and clean it. But there is no indication of whether or not these people had opted-in to the newsletter. Do you know?"

"I don't know. Just merge the lists."

"But Tiffany, you know that is against company policy. If they haven't opted-in to the corporate list, then we have to send them a special email with the offer to subscribe."

"I know the rules, Valerie."

"Then how can we find out?"

"Look, we weren't sure, so we just merged the lists. Everything will be fine."

"Honest mistakes are fine, but I don't like doing something on purpose and calling it an honest mistake later. How about if I track down the source for these names and ask?"

"If we do that and they were not opted in for the corporate list, then we will have to send an email that will only pull a two percent response at best. I'll end up with twenty new names instead of a thousand. We need that bump."

"Do I have permission to check? I don't think it would take that many phone calls."

"Whatever. I don't care."

Friday Night

Brad sat on the floor of Valerie's apartment as usual. "We should congratulate Lynn tonight for resigning from her ministry before she even started."

"Yes, how did it go with your pastor?" asked Valerie.

"I left him a voicemail message and he called me later. He was confused that I said no but I was still eager to be a part of the church and enthusiastic about his teaching. He asked if he had to remind me that he was my spiritual authority and I told him I already knew that and that I was looking forward to the next sermon series. He sounded confused and said he wanted to talk further later," said Lynn.

"That had to feel pretty good, Lynn," said Valerie.

"I feel relieved."

"I had a disagreement with Stan," said Randall. "He wanted me to stack cans without checking the dented ones. I warned him about the health regulations and he actually backed down. I couldn't believe it."

"I brought up a possible corporate policy violation with Tiffany and she got upset," Valerie said. "It wasn't a big deal. We wouldn't have gotten into any serious trouble, but I didn't want to do something on purpose and then call it an honest mistake later. I realized that this was a matter of conscious and a matter of ethics. She was not happy about it but she let me check before moving ahead."

"I've been trying to figure out what it means to follow well at Riverview. I'm not a member, I just attend there. I go regularly in order to get spiritually recharged. But I'm not giving anything back. What do you guys think? Am I following well in this area of my life?" Brad asked.

"No, you are not following well at church. If everybody did what you are doing then no ministry would happen there. The congregation would flounder," said Randall.

"But Brad is already doing youth ministry 55 hours a week. How is doing more ministry going to help him? His life will be out of balance," said Lynn.

"Balance in life is important," said Brad.

"Well if we are worried about balance then how are we going to follow well in every area of life?" asked Randall.

"Good point, Randall. I wanted to follow well at work so I worked late every day this week, including tonight. That's why I'm still in my work clothes on a Friday night. If I worked this hard every week it would adversely affect my health and relationships," said Valerie.

"Now you know how I feel," said Brad.

"You are doing ministry as a career, Brad. Go ahead and count the first 40 hours as work but you should also be giving volunteer hours to your own organization. You ask your volunteers to give ten hours a week after they have finished their regular job, so you had better be working at least 50 hours a week or you won't be keeping up with your own volunteers," Randall said.

"So how do we find balance?" asked Lynn.

"I suppose we have to slack off in some areas in order to give more time to others," said Valerie.

"But Jack said to follow well in all roles in life," said Lynn.

"I don't think that's possible if you have a full-time job," said Valerie.

"This is what we have to discover next," said Brad. "How can we follow well and maintain balance in life?"

Sunday Afternoon

Betty greeted the group at the door with hand sanitizer and led them back to Jack's office. A tray with fresh vegetables and dip filled the center of the table. "Sit down and dig in," said Jack. "Let's hear your reports."

"Well, we are all following better," Brad began. "Learning about the three types of followership really helped."

"We aren't just doing what our leaders tell us to do, we are doing what is right and helping them do what is best," said Valerie.

"I told Stan we needed to follow a food-handling regulation and he gave in to me," said Randall.

"Tiffany didn't want to check the status of an email list, but I insisted and she let me check it," said Valerie.

"I found the strength to tell my Pastor 'no' when I realized it was not a Type I followership issue," said Lynn.

Brad said, "We could see when we were doing each type of followership."

"That's good." Jack said. "Actually, you are always following in all three areas simultaneously. You are always following God. You are always a citizen of a country. In Type III, you usually have several roles where you are following leaders."

"Well that brings up another problem we are seeing, Jack. How can we follow well in all of these areas and maintain balance in life?" asked Valerie.

"Balance in life is important. But following well does not mean working harder. It doesn't mean putting in overtime. It doesn't have to take any extra time at all. Following well is a matter of thinking differently and seeing your leader and your role with fresh eyes," said Jack.

"But don't we have to slack off in some areas of life so we can follow well in others?" asked Brad.

"You don't achieve balance in life by following poorly," said Jack. He walked to the whiteboard. "You need to kick it up a notch. Tell me about the servants in the parable of the Ten Minas." He turned to draw another grid.

"Some guy leaves town to be crowned king and he gives ten of his servants one mina each to invest. When he returns, one servant earned ten minas, one earned five minas, and one gave him the mina back," said Brad.

"So did some of the servants follow better than the others?" asked Jack.

"Sure," said Valerie.

"Can we make the observation that there seems to be levels of followership?" asked Jack.

"That's obvious, I suppose," said Randall.

Let's turn to the parable in Luke 19. As they looked it up, Jack labeled the grid *Levels of Followership*. He numbered the rows one through five with five at the top and one at the bottom. "Read the verse about the servant who made ten times what he was given."

"That would be verse 16." Valerie read it.

> *The first servant reported, 'Master, I invested your money and made ten times the original amount!'*

"Where would you place him on this scale?" asked Jack.

"He would be the highest one," said Brad.

Jack wrote it on the top line. "How about the servant who made five times what he was given?"

"That's verse 18." Randall read it.

> *The next servant reported, 'Master, I invested your money and made five times the original amount.'*

"Where would this guy fall on the scale?" asked Jack.

"Next one down, he's a four," said Valerie.

"Who would like to read the verse about the wicked servant?" asked Jack.

"That would be verse 20." Brad read the verse.

> *But the third servant brought back only the original amount of money and said, 'Master, I hid your money and kept it safe.'*

"So where would he fit on this chart?" asked Jack.

"I'd put the slacker at level three," said Valerie.

"Let's think carefully. Could he have done any better?" asked Jack.

"Sure, he could have put it in the bank to collect interest," said Randall.

"Read that passage please," said Jack.

Randall found verse 23 and read it.

> *Why didn't you deposit my money in the bank? At least I could have gotten some interest on it.*

"Let's put this response as level three and the wicked servant at level two. Were there any servants who were worse yet?" asked Jack.

Nobody spoke. "Look at the last verse, verse 27," said Jack.

Brad read the verse.

> *And as for these enemies of mine who didn't want me to be their king—bring them in and execute them right here in front of me.*

"We'll put the enemies at level one," said Jack.

Then he stepped back to let them study the chart.

Levels of Followership

5	First servant earned 10 minas (v.16)
4	Second servant earned 5 minas (v.18)
3	Any servant could have earned some interest (v.23)
2	Wicked servant earned nothing (v.20)
1	Enemies rounded up to be killed (v.27)

"So now we have a simple scale here that illustrates different levels of followership. The better followers are towards the top and the poor followers are towards the bottom," said Jack.

"So what do we have to do to be at level five?" asked Brad.

"It's not so much doing as it is a way of being. It's about the quality of relationship that you have with the leader," said Jack. "It varies with the three types of followership. With Type I we can look at this way." Jack went up to the board and drew another grid.

Type 1 Followership

5	Wholehearted disciple
4	Growing disciple
3	Nominal disciple
2	Distracted disciple
1	Wayward disciple

"At level one are those who are far away from God. Level two are those who believe in Jesus but cares of this world or addictive behaviors are preventing growth. Level three are those who believe but who are investing the minimal amount of time and effort in spiritual matters. It's just not a priority for them. Level four includes those who are growing in faith and engaging in spiritual practices like Bible study, worship, prayer, and service. Level five includes those who are seeing more and more of their sinfulness, trusting in Christ more and more for forgiveness, and have a faith that expresses itself in love for God and others."

"This makes me uncomfortable. Isn't it a bit judgmental?" asked Lynn.

"It can be misused in a legalistic, judgmental way, Lynn. One always has to be careful about judging others," said Jack.

"You know," said Brad, "I can take every high school student I work with and easily place them on this scale without judging them. Our whole discipleship program is based on moving them up to mature believers with a faith strong enough to survive college. If we want to help them grow, then we have to start where they are at."

"Let's do another one." Jack drew a new grid.

Type II Followership

5	Activist citizen
4	Concerned citizen
3	Law-abiding citizen
2	Apathetic citizen
1	Lawless citizen

"When you are following Christ you are a disciple. When following the government your role is citizen. Level one are the criminals and those who violate the rights of others. Level two are those who don't care about politics or government and rarely bother to vote. Level three are those who quietly go about their lives and fulfill their basic duties as citizens. Level four are those who join in the conversation and actively participate in making government work. They stay informed and are not afraid to speak up. Level five include those who are working for positive change. They are enlisting others in important causes whether in the neighborhood or nationally."

"Anything wrong with being a three?" asked Valerie.

"No," said Jack.

"But wait a minute," said Randall. "Any healthy government requires concerned citizens to function or else it will fall apart. That takes more than a level three. In any neighborhood, if nobody is actively working to make the neighborhood a better place to live, then it will deteriorate. The world needs a whole bunch of fours and fives in order for the threes to survive."

"I suppose the key question here is whether or not you are the kind of person who wants to make the world a better place, even if only in some small way," said Brad.

"Yeah, are you a contributor or a consumer," said Randall.

"Let's move to levels of followership in terms of being on a team or following another human being." Jack drew a fresh grid and filled it in.

Type III Followership

5	Courageous follower
4	Engaged follower
3	Compliant follower
2	Disengaged follower
1	Disruptive follower

"At level one you have the followers who aren't following. They are causing problems for the leader and everybody else as well. Level two are those who are on the team but mentally checked out. You would put the slackers here. Level three are the followers who do everything they are told to do. They do their job, sure, but they are sheep. They are following but not following well. That's what levels four and five describe. Level four are those who are doing their part, encouraging everybody, supportive of the leader, and helping other followers along the way. Level five are those who are following well, helping other followers, and helping the leader to lead well. These are the people who have the courage to privately confront the leader or offer constructive feedback. At level five the follower has a sense of close teamwork with the leader."

"When you first started talking to us about learning how to follow, I assumed you were talking about level three," said Brad.

"So this is the difference between following and following well," said Valerie.

"This shows me how to take my game to the next level," said Brad.

"Let's get specific," said Jack. "What would it take to get to level four or five at work?"

"I know I'm not at level four," said Randall. "To follow better I would have to build a relationship with Stan. I would have to do more than work for him or report to him. I would have to work together with him. I would have to support him. I don't know if I can get there."

"You have to help him be successful, Randall. You would have to understand his job and the problems he is facing," said Jack.

"I can work on that."

"You can start by learning how to pronounce his last name."

"Are you serious? You are serious. I can work on that too I suppose," said Randall.

"I think my co-workers would put me at level four," said Brad. "We work together tightly. During this time when we have no executive director, I'm making sure that everybody has what they need to function. I don't know what else I could do to move it to a five."

"Seriously, you can't think of anything?" asked Jack.

"We don't have a director."

"Brad, do you pray for the board members?"

"I probably should do that more than I do." Brad hung his head slightly.

"Do you know them as individuals? Do you know anything about their families? Do you know anything about their own high school experience?"

"Not really."

"You can't have a good relationship with the board if you don't know the board members individually."

"So you want me to help the board to do their job?"

"That would be a level five response," said Jack.

"I think I would put myself at a three at work," said Lynn. "I do everything that Dr. Hanson says. I work diligently every day. We have problems in our procedures but that is not my job."

"Lynn, merely being a good worker bee is not following well. What else could you do?" asked Jack.

"I suppose I could tell Dr. Hanson about some of the problems, but he doesn't like to hear about things he can't fix immediately."

"If Dr. Hanson were doing his job and addressed these issues, what should he be doing?"

"He should be talking with everybody in the 'pit' and define the issues so we can change our procedures to streamline our systems."

"Good, then help him do that or just do it for him."

"Do part of his job?" asked Lynn.

"Yes, that's what level five sometimes entails."

"I can barely stand the thought of trying to make Tiffany successful," said Valerie. "She certainly is doing nothing to make me successful."

"That doesn't much matter," said Jack.

"Well, I can work on it. But it would involve me learning more about branding and online marketing. I would have to do some serious study in a few areas."

"Didn't you say that you were stuck at work and you wanted to move your career ahead? Become a good marketer. Learn to work well with Tiffany. Help her do her job. Your path forward goes through her office."

"All of you need to work on your relationship with your supervisor. It's not that you have to become best buddies. It's about how you interact and work together. At level one, the follower is resistant or antagonistic toward the leader. At level two, the follower is not working against the leader but is distant or disconnected. At level three, the follower is following the leader and meeting expectations. At level four, the follower develops a sense of teamwork with the leader. The follower is helping others to follow well. At level five, the follower develops a synergy with the leader. The follower is helping the leader to lead well. If you are following well, you will always be at levels four or five."

"What if your boss doesn't like you?" asked Valerie.

"You still have a working relationship. You can still do your part. You can still help others follow and you can still help the leader to lead well. You cannot blame your boss if you are not following well."

"What about following well at church? I can't figure that out what that means for me," said Brad.

"Who are you following?" asked Jack.

"I don't know."

"What does that tell you?"

"It tells me I don't even know where to start," said Brad.

"Well aren't you following Jesus?" asked Valerie.

"So this falls into Type I followership," said Lynn.

"But it's Type III followership too," said Randall. "I'm following my team leader when we setup and tear down."

"Following well at church involves both kinds of followership. Your first concern should be that you are growing as a disciple. So you should seek out what you need. One might need a small group, recovery group, or Bible study, and another might need an opportunity to serve. Everyone needs to engage with the Bible. First make sure you are following Jesus well. Then if you are part of a ministry team, follow well on that team. Strengthen your relationship with that leader who is another human being you are following at church."

"I go to church to recharge my spiritual batteries," said Brad, "I like being anonymous there."

"Brad, it sounds like you go to church but you are not plugged into the body of believers there," said Jack. "You don't have to volunteer for other ministries. Just figure out how to plug in there in a meaningful way."

"I want to serve somewhere at church. I need to be doing something. I just don't know where. I suppose I can start looking," said Lynn.

"I'm already following a leader at church. To follow well, I will need to talk to my team leader and the pastor about some adjustments we should make to improve what we do. Right now I'm just allowing the frustration build on the team," said Randall.

"I'm connected with a lot of families at my church. We are so small that you can't help getting to know people. But that also means we don't have many service opportunities that would make use of my strengths and gifts. So what can I do?" asked Valerie.

"Duh, volunteer for another ministry in the community. Would you like to invest ten hours a week working with youth at Suburban Life?" asked Brad.

"Some people volunteer in their church and others volunteer in the name of their church. You can follow well either way. If you find another place to serve in the community you should consider yourself a deployed volunteer," said Jack.

"I think we all know what we need to work on," said Brad.

"Yeah, this is going to be a rough week at work," said Randall.

"Your assignment is follow at level four or five in every area of your life. Keep making your journal entries. Don't forget about the being side of followership," said Jack.

"Jack, this is getting harder every week. Why do you always give us such challenging assignments?" asked Valerie.

Jack leaned back in his chair and smiled. "The more you sweat in peacetime, the less you bleed in war."

8

Monday Morning

Randall poured a cup of coffee and walked over to where Stan was sitting. He was studying papers on his clipboard and carefully crossing items off his list.

"How are you doing today, Stan?"

"Fine." Stan did not bother looking up from his work.

"Hey, Stan, I've got a question. How do you pronounce your last name?"

Stan looked up from his clipboard and looked at Randall's face. "What for?"

"I don't know. I'd just like to be able to pronounce your name."

"It's Sczcepansky."

"Whoa, slow down a bit."

Stan spoke slowly, "Shte-pan-sky."

"Shta-pan-sky."

"Shte!"

"Shte-pan-sky."

"Close enough."

"That's an uncommon name."

"Not in Poland."

"Did you grow up there?"

"I was born there and we immigrated to the US when I was eight."

"Was it hard to learn English?"

"I remember it was kind of scary. But if you want to play with the other kids you have to learn their language."

"Was school hard for you then, too?"

"I got caught up by high school."

"That must have been tough on you growing up?"

"Life is tough, you know."

Lynn knocked on Dr. Hanson's door. He opened it and said, "I didn't call for you."

"I know Dr. Hanson. Excuse me for bothering you, but I had an idea I wanted to run past you. I think we could probably make some simple changes in our procedures that would streamline our process and reduce the number of problems you have to deal with on a weekly basis. Is it all right if I pulled some small groups of employees together to see if we can identify the problems and some good solutions?"

He frowned and asked, "What changes are you going to make?"

"None. We are going to bring all the ideas to you and you can decide which would be wise to implement. Would you like to sit in on the meetings, too?"

"No, I've got too much to do."

"So it's okay for me to talk with the other staff?"

"I suppose, but don't make any changes without consulting me. Our current procedures developed over time for a reason."

"I'll keep you informed every step along the way."

Tiffany came by Valerie's cubicle and leaned against the wall. "Let's drop the new offer to our core list on Tuesday morning."

"Sounds good, Tiffany. I will do a quick test, proof the email, and then push it out."

"Thanks."

"Tiffany, as long as we are sending this offer to the core list, would it be a good idea to send the same offer to our small office and the home office lists? The price point would be in their range."

Tiffany paused and looked at a far point across the room. Then she looked at Valerie and said, "That's a good idea, let's do it."

"Do you want me to put different codes on them so we can track the responses separately?"

"That's a good idea, too."

BRAD WAITED AT THE COFFEE SHOP FOR the Suburban Life board chair. He was early on purpose. Mark Sonnenberg walked in three minutes ahead of schedule. "Brad, you beat me here."

"Hi Mark, good to see you."

"Thanks for meeting me in town. This is an easy walk from my office. Let me buy you some coffee."

They chatted about work and ministry while waiting for their order. When they got settled at a table, Mark asked, "So what do you have for me today?"

"Because we don't have an executive director at the moment, I pulled together the other staff and we laid out our ministry plan for the next school year. It's all in here." Brad slid the document across the table.

"Brad, I'm so impressed by the staff to do this planning on their own initiative. Thank you for keeping the board informed. As a board, we were afraid that you all would be rudderless heading into the new school year without an executive director. This will do a lot to reduce the anxiety we are feeling as a group right now."

"Also, I was wondering if you would want to meet like this for coffee every week. I can keep you updated on what is happening in the ministry. I can bring messages from the board back to the staff. We are all praying for the board as you do your search for the new director."

"That would help me immensely. Let's meet every week for the next few weeks."

"So, tell me about your children, Mark. Are they, like, my age?"

Friday Night

Brad sat on the floor in his usual spot. "Let's begin by sharing what we've been learning about followership."

"I've started praying for Stan. I don't know why I never thought of that the entire first year I worked with him. He's got three young daughters. He spends every weekend with them and his extended family. I realize that I have been viewing him as a boss instead of a human being."

"Does he still call you dipstick?" asked Valerie.

"Of course. But it doesn't bother me as much now."

"I've been pulling together groups of three or four women to talk about our procedures in the office. I was nervous about how they might react. I just coordinate a long coffee break with them and then ask them about all the problems they are experiencing with our current procedures. When I started viewing this as helping Dr. Hanson do his job, it felt more comfortable for me to bring people together," said Lynn.

"I've never done any thinking about how to make Tiffany successful. Now I think about it a lot. Before, all I thought about was getting my work done and making my career successful," said Valerie.

"I was afraid of pulling the staff together and running a planning meeting with them. I didn't want them to react negatively. But I simply pointed out that the board was flying blind and we needed to give them some information about how we were doing without an executive director. I also told them we needed to get involved in the process somehow so we could warn them if we thought they were making another hiring mistake like they made with Nick. We had no problem working together to draft the ministry plan."

"We are all making good progress on followership," said Randall. "I think it's time that we ask Jack to take us to the next level and start teaching us about leadership."

Brad looked at the two girls, "Is everybody ready to take it to another level?"

"I'm ready," said Valerie.

"Sure, I'll come along, but don't expect me to want to be a leader anytime soon," said Lynn.

"We need to stick together on this," said Brad.

Valerie raised her fist in the air and said, "Vamos!"

Sunday Afternoon

When everyone was seated around the table at Jack's home office, Jack walked back to the kitchen and returned with two pitchers, one with chilled lemonade with lemon wedges on the rim and the other with sun-brewed tea.

"You can have some lemonade, iced tea, or blend them together to make your own Arnold Palmer," said Jack. "I'm ready to hear about your week. Don't skimp on the juicy details."

Brad told about pulling the staff together to plan the year and setting up a regular meeting time with the board chair. "Following well was a lot more involved than I thought. I realized that I had to quit ignoring the board of directors. Having coffee with the board chair is easy. The hard part was simply recognizing the inadequacy of my behavior. I was doing everything I was expected to do but I wasn't following well and I didn't even realize it."

"Yeah, if you do five percent more as a follower you look like a genius," said Jack.

Lynn told about how scared she was to knock on Dr. Hanson's door and how she simply smiled and asked his permission to work on an obvious problem. She also told about pulling small groups of coworkers together. "I wasn't acting like the leader. I simply asked what problems they saw and took notes. Everybody had plenty to say when they realized I was listening carefully to them and cared about their opinions."

Randall told about asking Stan how to pronounce his last name. "I never thought of this guy as being a part of an extended family that got together every Sunday or of him having three daughters that look up to him and love him. By praying for him, I'm seeing a different side of him, I'm seeing him as a whole person, and I think he can sense that."

Valerie told about trying to anticipate what Tiffany would need and trying to make her successful. "The hardest part was actually wanting to see her succeed. At first I just went through the motions and then later my attitude came around."

"Once again, excellent work. You all are making real progress in followership," said Jack.

"So we think we are ready to move on to leadership," said Randall.

"Yes, we are itching to move on to the doing side and being side of leadership," said Brad.

Jack sat looking at them with a puzzled expression, then slowly looked at each individual for a short moment.

"Jack, we think we are ready to move on," said Valerie. "Do you think we are ready?"

Jack slowly shook his head. "Don't you see it?" he asked.

"See what?" said Randall.

"Don't you see the connection between leadership and followership?"

"Well, you taught us that good followers make good leaders," said Brad.

"We can see that you have to be a follower first. Now we want move on," said Valerie.

Jack leaned forward slightly and spoke in a soft voice. "You don't move on from followership. You are always going to be a follower. You can never forget that. But don't you see that you are already leading? Can't you see that leadership and followership are two sides of the same coin?"

"I'm not seeing it," said Randall.

"To follow well, you want to be REAL. Don't you also want your leaders to be REAL? Don't you want them to be responsible and think ahead? Don't you want them to be ethical at all times and treat people fairly? Don't you want an authentic and genuine relationship with them? Don't you want them to remain humble? Don't you want them to show love and kindness?" asked Jack.

"I can see how the being side of leading and following are connected," said Brad.

"Who you are on the inside leaks out to how you lead on the outside," said Jack.

"It makes sense that if you appoint someone to a leadership position who avoids responsibility, treats people unfairly, puts herself above others, is unloving and mean, then you are just asking for trouble," said Lynn.

"The essence of leadership is helping others follow well. If you don't know how to follow well yourself you cannot lead others to do so. Leaders lead and follow at the same time. A supervisor leads a team, but he or she follows a manager. You can't stop following well as you lead."

"Sure, you are following some people while leading others," said Valerie.

"Yes, but there is more. A good leader leads some of the time. Team members step up and they lead some of the time. Some have expertise and the team leader needs to follow their lead. A good leader follows the people he is leading. The best teams have a special synergy between the leader and the followers."

"You mean good teamwork?" asked Brad.

"You're getting warmer," said Jack. He got up from his chair and went to the whiteboard. "You don't yet fully grasp the leader-follower dynamic." He pulled the cap off a marker and paused staring at the blank whiteboard. Then he wrote *Theology of Leadership* and underlined it.

Jack turned toward them and asked, "Who was the first leader in the Bible?"

"Moses? No, Abraham!" said Brad.

"Noah?" said Randall.

"Uh, the guy who built the tower of Babel?" asked Valerie.

"No," said Jack, "God. In the beginning God was leading Adam. This is the first example of leadership and followership. God gave Adam work to do. He asked him to tend the Garden of Eden. He told him what was out of bounds. They communicated with each other.

"The second example is Adam and Eve. As Eve started helping Adam, he naturally led her. Adam and Eve experienced perfect harmony. Their relationship was so close that it was characterized by oneness. This same sense of oneness is what characterizes a perfect relationship between leader and followers. I call it the leader-follower dynamic.

"This kind of leading and following is so smooth that it is like ballroom dancing. One partner is the leader and the other is the follower, but they glide across the floor as one unit. It's difficult to observe who is leading and who is following. We only get brief glimpses of this kind of leadership today.

"You see, leadership was God's idea. He created it to function perfectly, and it did until sin entered the world." He turned back to the white board and wrote a few more words. Then he drew some arrows and the diagram looked like this:

Theology of Leadership

Perfection   Perfection

↘   ↗

Brokenness   Restoration

↘   ↗

Redemption

"Everything about leading and following became distorted after the fall. It had been ruined by sin. The perfect leader-follower dynamic became corrupted with everything else in the world. What used to be easy and natural became difficult. Selfishness, mistrust, and anger emerged. Leaders put themselves above others. Followers rebelled. Those in charge resorted to power and force. Follower abuse became the norm.

"We see so much bad leadership around us today because leaders are sinners, too. They are in need of salvation and the empowering work of the Holy Spirit to make them better people. They are often weak on the being side of leading and following. We live in a fallen world, and as a consequence the leader-follower dynamic is broken.

"Then Jesus was sent by God into the world to save the world. Because of the work that Jesus completed on the cross, we can be reconciled with God. This allows us to become followers of Jesus. He saves us, implants a new nature, and gives us the Holy Spirit to transform our lives. We can then become better followers because we are better people. Jesus also gave us an example of what perfect leadership looks like so we can become better leaders.

"We catch a glimpse of that perfect leader-follower dynamic when Jesus called his disciples. He walks along the shore, stops, looks, and says, 'Follow me.' The individuals immediately drop their nets and follow him. It doesn't last long because the disciples quickly fall out of step. But we see traces of it in the Bible. We also catch glimpses of it in the world from time to time.

"As disciples of Jesus, we have been given a new nature and the transforming power of the Holy Spirit. As we are formed more and more like Jesus, we become the kind of people others want to follow. In this way, we become better leaders and followers.

"Yet we continue to struggle against sin. We need to continually put off the old self and put on Christ. Placed in leadership positions, we encounter new temptations we must struggle to resist. So we are imperfect people leading imperfect followers and leadership remains difficult and follower abuse still happens.

"Every once in a while we see leaders and followers who really click, like a championship sports team or a high-performing work group. Or we see a leader who captivates us and we willingly join his tribe or follow digitally. By God's grace good leadership still happens, but even these instances are only a grainy photocopy of the leader-follower dynamic that God originally created.

"One day all believers will join God in heaven, and the leader-follower dynamic will be fully restored. It will be perfect once again. God will be leading his people and we will be following perfectly. We don't really know whether people will be leading and following each other in heaven and we can't know about that before getting there. But we know for sure that if we are leading each other, we will be experiencing that same perfect leader-follower dynamic that God intended in the beginning.

"He created it to be perfect, it was corrupted by sin, and he will make it perfect once again. That's the story of leadership, from beginning to end," Jack said.

"This is beautiful, Jack," said Lynn. "If this is how the leader-follower dynamic is supposed to function, then I don't care if I'm the leader or the follower."

"This means you don't need a position to lead, you can lead from anywhere," said Valerie.

"This means leadership is not about controlling others," Brad added. "It's about helping the leader-follower dynamic to happen."

"I need some more time to think," said Randall.

"Good. Reflect on your own experience for a moment. When have you observed the leader-follower dynamic working well?"

"I was on a summer mission trip in high school," said Lynn, "and we had these cool parents leading our group. Everybody meshed tightly and we would all pitch in to do the work. The parents didn't treat us like kids. We would work together all day and talk together in the evenings. We got a lot accomplished and we felt like a family."

"I experienced it my senior year of college," said Brad. "Our basketball coach brought us together and we were able to set ego aside. We melded as a true team that passed the ball well and executed with precision. The leadership on the floor would rotate easily between teammates. We would get on streaks where it felt like time slowed down. It was like the basketball was in control and making itself flow from one player to another. The coach was not on the floor but he created the conditions for it to emerge."

"I was in a group that had to write a paper together. I always hated group assignments because I could get better grades working alone," Randall said. "There would always be one or two people who didn't do their part and the rest of us would have to do extra. But this time we all clicked. One of the students emerged as the leader and got us organized. He assigned one guy to do nothing but compile the bibliography. We met at the library every day to check in and everything just clicked. Our paper was so much higher quality than any of us could have done alone."

"One summer I worked in an ice cream shop," said Valerie. "We had an outgoing college-aged manager. He got all the employees together at the beginning and helped us get to know each other. Then he said, 'How about if we have some fun this summer!' He showed us how to delight our customers. It was great. We were all focused on providing an enjoyable experience for our customers. It was like a game to see who could wow the most customers. He was clearly the manager but we never felt like mere employees."

"What about you, Jack?" asked Randall. "When have you caught a glimpse of the leader-follower dynamic?"

Jack leaned back in his chair and looked toward the ceiling. "I've seen it most frequently in ODAs."

"What are ODAs?" asked Valerie.

"Operational Detachment Alphas," said Jack, still looking up towards the ceiling.

"What are those?" asked Lynn.

Jack sat up his chair as if awakened from a dream. "I'm sorry, in the Army Special Forces, soldiers are deployed in twelve-man teams called Operational Detachment Alphas. The members of each ODA train intensively for any mission. They fight as one unit. We usually did short-duration strikes. I vividly remember one ODA in particular. I was the Non-Commissioned Officer in Charge. Whenever anyone would show leadership in some small way, like offering to go into a building first for example, the others would respond by saying, 'Go for it, I've got your back.' That phrase came to symbolize for me what I now call the leader-follower dynamic. My men were following so well it was effortless to lead them. We functioned as a single organism."

"Did you experience something similar leading in ministry?" asked Valerie.

"Yes, I had one translation team of young adults. We met every Saturday to do our work. We would read completed chapters aloud and anyone could raise their hand to suggest an improvement. We often had deep discussions to determine how to render difficult phrases. It was like we were thinking together. Different people would take the lead at different points of the discussion. Sure, I was the leader, but it felt like I was being carried along by the translation process at times."

"Which is more difficult, leading in the military or leading in ministry?" asked Randall.

"Both." Jack smiled slightly. "The military is a high-authority setting and a lot of ministries are low-authority. Missionaries have to raise their own support, so they often behave more like volunteers or independent contractors. In organizations with high-authority cultures you can get away with mediocre leadership by leaning on power and authority. In low-authority cultures all you have is leadership and individual relationships with those you supervise. It still boils down to leading other human beings in either setting, so there are more similarities than differences. Low-authority organizational cultures require higher levels of leadership."

"How do we help the leader-follower dynamic to occur?" asked Brad.

"That's the right question because that is going to be your assignment for the next few weeks."

"But Jack, we are not in charge. How can we help the leader-follower dynamic to occur?" asked Valerie.

"You start by following well. Then look for ways to remove anything that is getting in the way. Lead when you have something to offer."

"But nobody is asking us to lead," said Randall.

"Leaders don't wait to be asked. Sheep wait to be asked. If you have been following well then your leadership is more likely to be welcomed when your opportunity to contribute appears," said Jack.

"But we don't have a position," said Lynn.

"I'm not asking you to become the leader. I'm asking you to practice leading from where you are. Your goal is not to take over from the leader, but to help the leader-follower dynamic to occur by following well and leading in spurts."

9

Monday Morning

Brad walked into the Suburban Life office and straight back to the meeting room. The other staff members were already in place for the weekly staff meeting busily checking email. After Joe opened in prayer, Brad said, "I've got a message from the board for all of us. They are impressed with how well we are working together without a full-time director. They want to offer their congratulations to us on the annual ministry plan. So we should feel pretty good about that."

Bob asked, "Brad, why are you wasting so much of your time with the board of directors?"

"I'm just trying to follow well. I'm trying to help the board get the information they need to do their job and oversee our work."

"Can't they do their work without our help?" asked Mary.

"Look, somebody has to keep the board chair informed. Technically, Mark is the acting Executive Director until they find somebody for the position," said Brad.

"Well, I suppose you can spend your free time anyway you want," said Joe.

"Thank you for your enthusiastic support," said Brad. "I can't wait to deliver another affirming message from the board. Let's move on to the next agenda item."

Late Tuesday morning, Lynn sent an email message to the other seventeen office staff working in the 'pit.' The message asked for volunteers to form a special task force to study workflow processes. She made sure to mention that this task force was pre-approved by Dr. Hanson.

After coming back from eating lunch out with a friend from school, her inbox was filled with replies. Most were terse: "No thanks," "Not interested," "Good luck with that project," "Sounds like a lot of work making recommendations that will never get implemented," "I regret to inform you that I will not be available for the aforementioned special task force."

Lynn placed her hands on her cheeks and rested her elbows on her desk. "What's the matter Lynn?" asked Sylvia.

"Leadership is harder than I thought."

"What do you mean?"

"I just sent out an email about the task force and all of them are coming back negative."

"Oh, I said no, too."

"Why?"

"Sounded boring. Nothing against you."

"It's hard to lead when nobody will follow," said Lynn.

Randall entered the front door of Faith Bible Church and saw the sign: *Visit our newest site in Hillcrest*. He made his way to the meeting room and greeted the other members of the core volunteer team.

Pastor Steve opened the meeting with a short devotional on waiting on the Lord. The first agenda item was decline in offerings. That led to a discussion about decline in attendance. Some started to blame the worship team. The worship leader blamed the auditorium. "It's not conducive," he said. The setup and tear down people said it was the best location currently available in the Hillcrest area.

Randall raised his hand to speak. "You know, there are some things we can change and there are some things we can't change. I think it would be better if we focused on the things that we can change. For example, 9:30 is an odd starting time. What if we pushed it back a half hour and started the service at 10:00?"

"We're not changing the start time," said the worship leader.

"Randall, we risk creating conflict in the church if we would try to change the worship time," said Pastor Steve. "Let's just keep things as they are and just try a little harder and see if it doesn't turn around."

TIFFANY STOPPED BY VALERIE'S CUBICLE and asked for ten copies of the monthly sales report.

"Tiffany, while you are here, I have an idea that I thought might help the department run a bit smoother. I was wondering about calling a meeting with us and some of the software programming managers to improve communications and help us understand the new products releasing in the near future. Our company is a bit siloed, you know. It might even be a benefit to the whole company by breaking down some of the barriers between departments. If it works, it could make you look good to upper management."

Tiffany stiffened. "There is no way—repeat, no way—that I'm going to have 'propeller-heads' coming over here and telling me how to do my job." She looked at Valerie, "What's the matter, you don't have enough to do in marketing so you want to go visit all the other departments and see what they do all day? We'll do our job, let's just hope that they do theirs and give us decent product to sell."

She turned to walk out then paused and turned back. In a fake sweet voice she said, "If you want to meet cute tech guys, there are better ways to do that, sweetie."

Sunday Afternoon

Jack walked into his office carrying a cutting board with a sausage on it and another plate with cheese and crackers. "I'm telling you right now this is good sausage. I picked it up in Milwaukee. Betty and I took a little day trip to Wisconsin. I'm fine if we eat the whole thing this afternoon. I bought it especially for this meeting. So what's up with you all?"

"Overall, we are doing better at following well. But we are having problems leading. We are making attempts to lead and we are all getting shut down," said Brad.

"Yeah, following well doesn't always bring the results you are looking for. Some situations and people are beyond your help," said Jack. "Tell me about what you were feeling on the inside."

"It hurts," said Brad. "The board just wants to stick me in the position and call it done. The other staff could care less about the board. If I were the new executive director I'm afraid they would start pulling away from me."

"I was in a meeting at church hearing about giving and attendance patterns. I suggested focusing on things we could change instead of complaining about things we couldn't change. Pastor Steve seemed fine with the complaining but shut down the conversation when I recommended adjusting the worship time," said Randall.

"How did it feel?"

"It felt like he cut me off at the knees."

"I tried to lead by forming a task force to study our work flow processes. I invited everybody in our area. Nobody said yes. Half said no and half didn't bother replying. I told you I wasn't a leader," said Lynn.

"How did it feel?"

"It felt like everybody hated me."

"I was trying hard to make Tiffany successful and offered what I thought was a great idea. She really let me have it. I felt like going back to following poorly."

"Well, sounds like everyone has been hurt this week," said Jack.

"It's the same every week, Jack," said Brad.

"Except it's getting worse as we try harder to follow well," said Valerie.

"Trying to lead takes the pain to another level," said Randall.

"Yeah, it's like that," said Jack. "I know it's hard. That's why I can tell you are doing a good job at following well. It sounds like you are at the next turning point. So do you want to quit now and thank me for the free coaching or do you want to slay the dragon?"

"What dragon?" asked Lynn.

"When it comes to leading other people, everybody is afraid of something. It might be a fear of conflict, a fear of disapproval, a fear of being criticized, being excluded, or not doing it perfectly. Whatever fear is holding you back from leading in short spurts is your dragon to slay. If you follow well and slay the dragon, then you can lead."

Jack cut some more sausage for them. "Hey this tastes like it could have come from a dragon, what do you think?"

"I can feel the dragon, Jack. I feel it every time I try to help the other staff follow well. How do you slay one?" asked Brad.

"You have to face your inner fear, call it what it is, and stare it down. Let's spend some time talking and see if we can't help each other identify their fear. What are you afraid might happen?"

"I don't want the staff to think less of me. I don't want them to exclude me. I need them to want to hang out with me. I want them to treat me like a friend, not a boss," said Brad.

"Okay, so you are the kind of person who needs and wants the approval of others. You are a people person. You fear disapproval. Is fear of disapproval your dragon to slay?" asked Jack.

"That's it. You hit it dead on."

"I don't want to be wrong, ever," said Randall. "I keep second-guessing my own ideas. What if it's not the best solution? Plus I keep wondering if I'm leading the right way. It gets me tied up into knots. I don't sound insecure but sometimes I feel that way."

"So you like to be right. You fear being wrong."

"Yeah, my dragon is fear of being wrong or doing it the wrong way."

"Mine is easy," said Lynn. "I'm a marshmallow when it comes to conflict. I like harmony in relationships. I'd rather just go along with what other people want."

"Sounds like fear of conflict is your dragon to slay," said Jack. "If it makes you feel any better, that is a common one."

"I'm afraid of rejection like everybody else of course, but that's not the biggest fear. It's more a reluctance to take responsibility for my life. I'm floating along in life and letting things happen to me. That's why I'm stuck at work and I'm stuck at church. I'm blaming the company for not plotting a course for my career and I'm silently blaming the priest for not having a ministry that fits me," said Valerie.

"You are afraid to be assertive," said Jack.

"I don't even like to use the word."

"Being assertive is not being aggressive. Being assertive is simply telling people what you think and what you need and want. It is not aggressively trampling over the rights of others and it is not being passive and letting others trample over you," said Jack.

"That's my dragon," said Valerie.

"Well, good work. Thank you for your willingness to be vulnerable today. We were able to isolate the dragons quickly because of the hard work you have been doing in trying to follow well. I know you all have a lot to think about."

"Same assignment?" asked Brad.

"Yes, but with a twist. Follow well, slay the dragon, lead in short bursts, and find new ways to help the leader-follower dynamic to occur."

10

Monday Afternoon

Sylvia walked into the lunch room and saw the enormous piece of paper taped to the wall with boxes, diamonds, and arrows all over it. "What in the world are you doing, Lynn?"

"Oh, I'm just mapping our work processes."

"Well, what are all of these boxes?" Sylvia asked.

"This is an attempt to trace all the steps in billing Medicare and non-Medicare patients and their insurance companies. I'm a bit overwhelmed by all the steps and loops," said Lynn.

"Where am I on here?" Sylvia asked. Her question began a fifteen-minute conversation that improved and detailed a part of Lynn's huge diagram.

Tina came into the lunchroom. "What are you guys doing?"

"Hi Tina, would you like to help?"

Over the course of two days all seventeen employees had looked over the chart of steps and made corrections when some of their work was not adequately noted. The chart grew in complexity and began to overwhelm the entire workgroup. Some started noting whole loops that could be cut out by getting sign offs from nurses earlier in the process. Lynn noted these changes with green dotted lines. She was getting the employees to see the whole process instead of just their small part in it. The same employees who didn't want to be a part of the task force were now coming to her with suggestions for process improvements.

Randall walked into the store manager's office and shook his hand firmly. "Hi Vic, are you having a good day?"

"You bet, Randall. Thanks for stopping in. Have a seat." Vic pointed him to a chair. "Hey, Stan is speaking highly of you recently. Other employees in the store have gone out of their way to say good things about you too. It's unusual for an employee to kick it into another gear after two years in the same job. I wanted you to know that we all like what we are seeing."

"Thank you very much, I'm just trying to do my job and follow well."

"I also want you to know that there will be more opportunities for you to apply for a management position later this year. Several of our stores have managers ready to retire."

"Thank you. I'm working on developing my leadership skills so I'm ready."

"I have a position opening up. Would you like a transfer to dairy? The pay is the same of course. A little job rotation is a good thing if you are on the management track. It keeps work from getting boring. I'm well aware that your current supervisor is not the easiest guy to work for, Randall. I can move you next week if you want it."

"Thank you again, Vic, I really appreciate the offer. However, I think I would prefer to stay with Stan until I might qualify for an open management position."

"Are you sure, Randall?"

"Yeah. But thank you for the offer. I appreciate that you considered me for it."

VALERIE RODE INTO THE CITY WITH THREE other women from church. They were driving to a shelter for battered women where they served as volunteer staff. They came in every Saturday because Saturdays were always busy days for intake. This was her first time to see the shelter. Donna, the Director of Development, gave her a tour of the facility. She met several of the residents, one with three young children clinging to her jeans. Up in the reception area, two young women brought their friend who still had blood crusted in her hair from the beating she received the previous night.

"So this is going to be your job on Saturdays, Valerie, manning the front desk and the phone. We have strict procedures about information that we can and cannot give out. They will train you well for the position. Do you have any questions?"

"Yes, tell me about your role and what you do in development?"

Donna gave her a detailed listing of all her duties including special events, major donor appointments, newsletters, and writing grant proposals.

"Do you use email to keep in touch with your donors?"

"No, we haven't gotten into that yet. We have a lean staff here for all the services we provide, as you can tell."

"Donna, would you like a volunteer to help you in development? I could assist with PR, writing articles for the newsletter, and setting up an email strategy. I'd love to use my marketing skills to help you keep in touch with your donors. I could ride in every Saturday with the others so we could work together and I could do some writing for you in the evenings."

"That would be awesome! We'll find somebody else to man the front desk." said Donna.

BRAD WENT TO THE OFFICE EARLY AND waited for the others to arrive for the Wednesday morning staff meeting. After opening prayer, Brad said, "I've got an idea and I'd like you guys to join me in it."

"Now what?" said Bob.

"The board is getting discouraged. How about if we all go to the next board meeting and give them a dog and pony show. Let's tell them some recent ministry stories. Let's thank them for volunteering their time and joining us in this important mission. And let's pray for each of them one at a time. What do you say?"

"We'd have to cancel our Thursday evening meetings," said Mary.

"Yes, one time can't hurt. Or, you could let your volunteers take the steering wheel for one night."

"Why should we worry about the board?" asked Bob.

"Because they are our board Bob," said Beth. "They are partners with us in our mission. They are donors and volunteers in our organization."

"Well, if we are all going to do it together then it doesn't sound that bad," said Mary.

"Let's keep it to an hour. We can each lead part of the meeting. What else can we do to bless our board members?"

Sunday Afternoon

Betty greeted the four at her front door and gave each of them a warm hug. She motioned for them to head toward Jack's office.

"Are you forgetting the anti-bacterial gel?" asked Lynn.

"Oh, the doctor said we don't need to worry about that anymore."

Jack welcomed everyone and had them take a seat at the table. He went back to the kitchen and returned with chips and salsa. "The green one is mild and the red is hot. I'm eager to hear about the fears you had to stare down this week."

"I'm afraid of conflict," said Lynn. "I was reluctant to recruit people for a task force for fear that some would be upset they were not selected. But I found a way around it. I got a large piece of paper and started mapping our processes in the lunchroom and invited others to join in. Instead of telling people what to do, I simply invited them to comment on what I had drawn on the wall and to add details about their own area. Tina said I was using a Tom Sawyer approach because I made the work look fun."

"That's leadership, Lynn," said Jack.

"I couldn't find a volunteer position that would make use of my strengths and gifts, so I proposed one and they went for it," said Valerie. "I couldn't believe it. I simply said what I wanted and it happened to be something they needed but hadn't realized it. Before, I would have simply served in the position they were offering. But I've decided to accept responsibility for my own life. Being assertive was hard but I simply put it out there and left the rest to God. I really enjoy working with Donna each Saturday."

"Taking responsibility is the R in REAL," said Jack.

"I was nervous about asking the other staff about joining me at the board meeting, but I made my reasons clear up front and they bought into it. I want people to like me, but I also want to see them grow. I'm learning that if I can stare down that fear of not being accepted by others I can be more effective. Going forward, I want to follow well whoever the board hires and help my student leaders and volunteers learn to follow well," said Brad.

"You are leading and following at the same time, Brad," said Jack.

"My fear is being wrong. When I faced it I realized I was making a huge mistake with my career direction. As a history major I had refined my research skills but I wasn't using them. I would not use them as a manager either. I applied to Natural Foods because of its high ranking on the best workplaces list and their benefits. I don't even like grocery stores. I decided I need to look for a new job. My need to be right was preventing me from seeing my mistake," said Randall.

"You used your research skills to find a job," said Jack. "What you need to do now is find a job that will let you use your research skills."

"Exactly! I don't know what kind of research jobs might be out there but I know how to find out," said Randall.

"Well, we have reached an important point in this coaching relationship. You are all ready to graduate," said Jack.

"But we have so much more to learn about leadership, we are just getting started," said Valerie.

"Yes, you have started," said Jack. "That was my job, to get you started. There are many leadership skills you have yet to master, but you can learn those without me."

"So that's it, we're done?" asked Randall.

"Well, I brought along a gift for each of you." Jack reached back to his desk and handed them a small laminated card.

"It's a job aid. This is a summary of the key points we covered over the past few months. Keep it with you or post it somewhere prominent so you will be reminded to continue following well."

"Thank you, Jack," said Lynn.

"I would also like it very much if each of you would keep me updated on how you are doing by email. I enjoy seeing the results of my labors you know."

"Sure, we'll do that," said Brad.

"But what about you, Jack, what are you going to do?" asked Lynn.

"I don't know. I feel good but I'm in a tough place. I'm not a good

Follow Well

- You learn to lead by learning to follow

- Do the inner work of getting REAL

- Differentiate between Type I, II, and III followership

- Strive for level four or five in all areas of life

- Leading and following are two sides of the same coin

- Create the conditions for a healthy leader-follower dynamic to occur

- The heart of leadership is helping others follow well

fit for most church staffs. Not many organizations want to hire a cancer survivor who is over 62 and forcibly retired from his last position. So I am waiting on the Lord."

"We'll promise to pray for you every Friday night," said Brad. "But you have to keep us informed, too!"

11

Over the Next Few Weeks

Brad was the first person to arrive to the Wednesday staff meeting at the Suburban Life office. He talked with Mary and Beth while they all waited for Bob and Joe to arrive.

"Welcome, guys, let's get started. Before we pray, I have this crazy idea that I want to share with you guys. We really have to put our heads together on this one. If you guys think this is a stupid idea I'll drop it right away."

"Well, let's hear it," said Joe.

"Okay, the board has not found anyone for the executive director role yet. At their next meeting they are going to vote on hiring a search firm to help them find somebody. So they are intent on getting somebody into that position soon. Now, what if they make another bad hire like Nick? Or worse?"

"That would be horrible. We're doing just fine without a director," said Beth.

"So here is my crazy idea. What if I took on the role?" Brad raised his eyebrows and waited.

"But we thought you preferred to work with youth," said Mary.

"I would stay directly involved with youth and volunteers but scale it back to half-time and use the other half-time for the Executive Director role. But I would need you guys 100 percent with me. If I can't get your full agreement and support, I'll drop the whole thing."

"It would be better to have you in the position rather than somebody who doesn't understand youth ministry," said Bob.

"I'm not going to start acting bossy or anything. We will remain peers. I'll be working in the ministry right alongside of you. The only difference is that I'll also be working with the board, our donors, and the bookkeeper. There may be times when I will have to make the final call, but I'll do everything I can to make this a great place to do ministry."

"We would still be involved in making decisions together?" asked Joe.

"Yes, just like we are making this one right now. For this to work, we have to continue to function as a team," said Brad.

AFTER THE WORSHIP SERVICE ENDED, Lynn walked to the children's ministry wing to find Susan, the Children's Ministry Director. Susan was greeting parents as they came to pick up their children. "Hi Susan, my name is Lynn Chiang."

"Hi Lynn, nice to meet you. How can I help you?"

"I'd like to set up a phone call with you. I'm looking for a way to get more involved at church. I'm a project person and I like organizing things. This ministry seems highly organized. I like little kids. Could I be useful to you as a volunteer?"

"Yes! I'd love to talk more with you, Lynn. We have an application process and background check but I'll tell you about that later. Can we meet for coffee this week?"

THE ADMISSIONS OFFICER OPENED HIS door and walked over to Valerie. "Hi, I'm Gary Richards, welcome to our university."

"Hi Gary, my name is Valerie Martinez."

"Come into my office." He left the door open and motioned for her to have a seat at his table. "So what program are you interested in?"

"I'd like to apply for the M.A. in marketing program."

"So, you've ruled out an MBA with a marketing emphasis?"

"Yes, I'm more interested in focusing on integrated marketing communications."

"Well, sounds like you've done your research. Why do you want a graduate degree?"

"I have to take responsibility for my own career. Nobody is going to do that for me. This is my next logical step to prepare myself for a more specialized marketing position. I want to be ready when a new opportunity comes along."

"Good. We'd love to have you in our program. You sound like a natural leader too."

PASTOR STEVE CALLED A SPECIAL MEETING of the core leadership team for Faith Bible Church at Hillcrest. "We need some new ideas. As you all know attendance is down, offerings are down, and now morale is down. We need to seek God's will."

"What's our average attendance?" asked one of the team members.

"It's now at 45 adults in worship."

"Didn't we have over 250 at our launch?"

"265."

"Do we have the potential to break even with our current offerings and expenses?" asked another.

"No, not even close. But we can expect continued financial support from Faith Bible for a few years. They are committed to multi-site ministry."

"Maybe we can do more praise and worship songs people already know," suggested a team member.

The worship leader responded glumly, "We could, but then we get criticized for doing 'old' contemporary music. Plus the songs no longer tie into the theme of the service."

Randall raised his hand to speak. "Are all options on the table?"

"Sure, we are desperate," said Pastor Steve. "We are open to anything God might have in mind for us."

"Well, here is an idea. Please take it for what it is worth. Why not shut it down, rebuild the core, and re-launch? I've been doing some reading on multi-site ministry. We have a couple of key problems here. One, Hillcrest is too close to Faith Bible Church. We all know families that went back to the central campus because of the expanded offering of programs. Two, we did not have a connection strategy. If we were going to have small groups, we should have built that up before the launch. Three, we rented unsuitable space because it was a bargain. If we close it now we will still have the financial resources to rebuild. If we let it straggle and drain our resources we may not have that option."

"Oh, that would be so hard," said Pastor Steve.

THE EIGHT BOARD MEMBERS OF SUBURBAN Life gathered at the office. Brad led them back to the meeting room and then Mark Sonnenberg led the group in a time of prayer. "Our first agenda item is whether or not to retain a search firm to help us find a new director."

"I have some relevant information to report on that," said Brad. "I might be willing to accept the position after all. I think it is possible to fulfill this role with half of my time and keep working with youth the other half. So I'm open to taking the position. But I can only accept it under certain conditions."

"Brad, we would love to hire you for the executive director role. But you said you didn't want it and you preferred to remain in a direct service role. What changed your mind?" asked Mark.

"I realized that I don't have to lead the way Nick did. I can lead using my strengths and gifts. Plus, Bob, Joe, Beth, and Mary pledged to be 100 percent with me on this. As I kept praying for our new director, I realized more and more that I could probably do the job."

"Can we simply take a voice vote now?" asked Mark.

"I said that I have some conditions," said Brad.

"Well, what are they?" asked Mark.

"I can only take this position and work with the board of directors if you guys step up your game, too."

"You've got our attention, Brad. Exactly what do you mean?" asked Mark.

"I can't lead the staff and pull this wagon too. You are going to have to get out and help push. We will have to work together as a team. I want a close relationship with my board. I need help thinking about our finances and our future. I expect near-perfect attendance at board meetings. I would expect every board member to be a generous donor to our organization. I would also hope that the board will manage itself and conduct an annual evaluation of board member performance. In other words, I want you to become a good board. Those are my conditions."

"Brad, if you wouldn't mind stepping outside we will need to go into executive session for a while, but please don't leave the building, we are probably going to want to continue this discussion," said Mark.

Friday Night

"Congratulations Brad! You got a promotion," said Randall.

"It's a demotion, Randall. A 50 percent demotion. I'm now a servant to those who are on the front line of ministry. How is your job search going?"

"I'm scheduled for my third interview with the documentary film company. It's so cool what they do. I would be the only researcher on staff. Much of my work would be working with outside experts on whatever documentary is in process."

"Lynn, did I hear you got promoted, too?" asked Brad.

"Not really. Dr. Hanson wanted me to implement all the changes in workflow processes that I recommended. He wanted to add some duties to it and make me office manager. I told him that was not the right solution. I asked him to simply move me into the new role without a title. So he did. I actually function more like an assistant to Dr. Hanson. We are solving so many problems at work that the other employees are grateful to me. It's great. I can help good things happen and I don't have to be the boss!"

"How do you like being a consultant, Valerie?" asked Lynn.

"It's not consulting. I'm just offering my marketing services to a couple other ministries now. It worked out so well helping Donna at the shelter, and I learned so much about connecting with donors. I thought I would offer to assist a few other choice organizations. Now, if I got paid for it then I suppose you could call it consulting."

"We are shutting down Hillcrest and rebuilding from scratch. How's Riverview doing, Brad?" asked Randall.

"Good. I found a way to plug into church. I meet for coffee with two businessmen who attend there. I'm taking them through a Bible study and they are mentoring me in how to lead staff, work with a board, and understand financial reports. It's a win-win."

"Any news from Jack?" asked Valerie.

"Nothing," said Brad.

"Let's send him a text message right now and thank him!" said Valerie.

"Do you think he's home on a Friday night?" asked Randall.

BETTY WAS SITTING IN THE LIVING ROOM reading a magazine when Jack's cell phone buzzed. She called out to him, "Jack, your phone!"

He walked into the living room and picked it up. "Ha! This is a text from Brad, Lynn, Randall, and Valerie. Listen to this. 'Jack, you were so right. Followership is the key to learning how to lead. Thank you for helping us learn to follow well.' "

"Jack, that's so nice," said Betty. "Maybe you should be doing more of this?"

"More of what?" asked Jack.

"More coaching like this. Maybe this is your next calling. Maybe this is what God has in mind for you next."

Jack stood silent for a moment. "Hmm, interesting thought."

"I think you would be good at it," said Betty.

Jack opened his phone and replied to the text message: *Keep moving forward, I've got your back.*

A CONCISE THEOLOGY OF LEADERSHIP AND FOLLOWERSHIP

In this story, four young adults seek guidance from a mentor to help them solve their problems at work and church. As they progress, they also develop a Biblical perspective on leadership and followership that transformed the way they interacted with their leaders. The Bible passages were all familiar to them. They simply had never made these connections before because their mental model of leadership was flawed. The mentor guided them to a new understanding of leadership by helping them learn to follow well first.

Most believers want the Bible to inform their thinking about leadership, but they struggle to make the connections to everyday leading and following. Prayerful reflection on what the Scripture has to teach us can adjust our mental model of leadership so it becomes easier to make these connections. Then it becomes easier to apply the Bible to our lives as we lead and follow others in all situations.

Thinking theologically about leadership can make us better leaders. For most of us, building a theology of leadership feels overwhelming. Where do we even begin?

One solid starting point is simply acknowledging that leadership is God's idea. The Lord is the creator and founder of leadership. He created human beings with the ability to lead and to follow.

If this is true, then leadership is not a human invention. It is not a necessary evil in a fallen world. It is not some kind of heavenly compromise. Leading and following was an intentional feature of God's creation. Many aspects of leadership are socially constructed, such as the difference between clear task direction and bossiness or offering advice and micromanaging. Despite obvious culture differences in leadership, all cultures have leaders and followers. The basic dynamics of leading and following remain remarkably consistent across cultures and through history. Groups of people may choose their own goals and develop differing social norms for acceptable leader behavior, but the phenomenon of leaders and followers working together toward meaningful goals is universal. Urges to lead and to be led well come as standard equipment in human beings.

God did not have to invent leadership. He could have created a world without a need for leaders where everyone would automatically coordinate their efforts with everyone else for mutual benefit—like ants or bees. He could have decided to lead the whole world himself directly. He could have decided to use plainly visible angels. Instead, in his infinite wisdom, he chose to have people lead each other in various ways. Leadership was not an afterthought at creation. It began in the mind of God before Adam and Eve were created.

This starting point, if we accept it, immediately leads to some troubling questions: If leadership is God's idea, then why doesn't it work better in daily life? Why do we have so many disappointing experiences of being led? Why is it so difficult to lead others? To answer those questions, we have to go back to the beginning.

Leadership when Everything was Perfect

In the beginning, leadership was created by God as a good and natural way for people to interact and function together. Leadership worked perfectly in the Garden of Eden, but it was corrupted by the fall into sin. So what we experience in daily life is leadership spoiled by sin. When leaders and followers are functioning well and everybody's efforts are meshing seamlessly, we get a partial glimpse of what leadership once was and how God intended it to function.

With only Adam and Eve in the Garden, how do we know that leadership existed before the fall? The first and most powerful example is easy to miss: God was leading Adam, and Adam was following God. This is the first instance of leadership and followership in human history. They communicated with each other. Adam walked with God in the cool of the day and they would talk together (Genesis 3:8-9). God gave him work to do in the Garden of Eden (Genesis 2:15). One of his tasks involved naming all the animals (Genesis 2:19-20). God told him what behavior was in bounds and out of bounds (Genesis 2:16-17). God initiated and Adam responded. God led, Adam followed.

Another instance of leadership and followership before the fall was in the relationship between Adam and Eve. God made Eve to be a helper suitable for him (Genesis 2:18). As Eve began to help Adam, Adam naturally led her. But this was not a bossy or domineering leadership that we frequently experience today. It was a kind of leadership that was unspoiled by sin. Adam did not say, "Shut up and do as I say, I'm in charge of this garden." Instead, he led Eve as God had been leading him. He walked and talked with her. He considered her a part of his own being (Genesis 2:23). Their relationship was so close that it was marked by oneness (Genesis 2:24). This same sense of oneness also marked the leader-follower dynamic that they shared. They were partners. They experienced perfect harmony. This kind of leadership functions so smoothly that, like two dancers gliding across a ballroom floor, it's difficult to tell who is doing the leading and who is doing the following. Today we only catch brief glimpses of this kind of leader-follower dynamic in action, if we see it at all.

Because leading and following occurred in the Garden of Eden, it was a part of God's creation from the start. But, along with all creation, leadership was ruined by the fall into sin.

Leadership after Being Ruined by the Fall

Everything about leadership became distorted after Adam and Eve sinned. The serpent came to Eve and twisted the truth about the fruit from the tree in the middle of the Garden. He told her she would not die but become like God knowing good from evil. Eve decided to try the fruit. Adam, who was right there with her, did nothing to stop her (Genesis 3:6). Adam failed to follow God and failed to lead his wife. This was the first leadership failure. Eve led the way by biting the fruit first. This was the second leadership failure.

Adam and Eve were ejected from the Garden and exiled to a fallen world. The relationship between them was no longer perfect. Their sin broke the oneness they experienced in leading and following. Adam blamed Eve for what had gone terribly wrong. Eve blamed the serpent (Genesis 3:12-13). Selfishness, anger, and mistrust emerged in their conversations. Leading and following wasn't smooth and effortless anymore. The beautiful leader-follower dynamic that God had created became corrupted along with all creation.

Eve would no longer experience the loving and flowing nature of leading and following with Adam. Instead, as God explained to her, "You will desire to control your husband, but he will rule over you" (Genesis 3:16). Their relationship after the fall would be something far less than she was used to experiencing. Leading and following would be made more difficult because of sinful desires and conflict.

Leading on an everyday basis would become more difficult for Adam. God told him, "The ground is cursed because of you. All your life you will struggle to scratch a living from it." (Genesis 3:17). Life would no longer be easy. Leading and following would no longer be as natural as breathing. Leadership would mutate and present continual challenges and daily annoyances.

This fallen leadership is what we see in the world today. Bosses treat workers harshly. Supervisors play favorites. Politicians misuse power. Coaches ignore certain players. Officials flaunt their authority. Rulers lord it over their people (Mark 10:42). The leader-follower dynamic that God created has been severely damaged.

Even with all the research and books available to us, leadership is still messed up. When managers or politicians or pastors dominate in meetings, demand their own way, treat people as objects, or abuse followers, we typically call them 'strong' leaders. Harsh leaders would be a better descriptor. Clumsy would work. Maybe we should describe them as completely inept at creating a healthy leader-follower dynamic. What we call strong leaders are just people using power or threatening followers or otherwise acting in an aggressive way. Why do we put up with it and call them 'strong' leaders as if what they are doing is acceptable? As followers, our mental model of leadership must be messed up, too.

The main reason we tend to have many instances of poor leadership today is that leaders are sinners, too (Romans 3:23). In their heart they are enemies of God (Colossians 1:21) and slaves to sin (John 8:34). Apart from Christ and without the help of the Holy Spirit, they may attempt to lead well, but human effort alone can only take them so far. They are easily ensnared by the fresh temptations that accompany certain leadership positions (James 1:14-15). To be better leaders, they first need to be better people. To become better people, they need a new nature, which is only available through the redemptive work of Christ (Titus 3:4-6).

Leadership Redeemed by Christ

Jesus came to seek and save those who were lost (Luke 19:10). Salvation comes through faith in Christ (Romans 10:9-10). Through God's grace, we receive forgiveness of our sins (Ephesians 1:7) and freedom from the power of sin (Romans 8:2). We become a new creation in Christ with a new nature (2 Corinthians 5:17). Conversion and regeneration has leadership implications. When we are no longer controlled by our sinful nature (Romans 8:9), we can lead more effectively. Christ gives us the inner strength we need to lead and follow well (Philippians 4:13).

Leadership has both a doing side and a being side. Business authors tend to emphasize the doing side—how to lead and what works. Religious authors tend to emphasize the being side—the character and heart of the leader that drive his or her actions. Most of the widely-accepted theories of leadership recognize the importance of both sides. The Psalms mention both sides speaking about King David: "He cared for them with a true heart and led them with skillful hands" (Psalm 78:72). The Bible is filled with wisdom and teaching about the being side of life. If we become better people, then we have the potential to become better leaders.

Jesus also provides us with the ultimate example of what it means to be a good leader. He loved us and gave himself up for us. Paul encourages us to follow his example (Ephesians 5:2). Because he lived a sinless life (Hebrews 4:15), he simply never made any leadership mistakes. That puts him in a category apart from any of the other great leaders throughout history. They all made plenty of leadership blunders. His leadership was unmarred by sin (1 Peter 2:21).

We catch a brief glimpse of what leadership was like before the fall when Jesus says, "Follow me" (Mark 1:17, Mark 2:14, John 1:43). The fishermen leave their boats, the tax collector leaves his booth, and others leave their home. They are captivated by him and, like a dance, they move with him as he moves. It's a short burst of leadership-followership marked by oneness. It doesn't last long, of course, because the disciples quickly fall out of step. Jesus leads so effortlessly that we have difficulty seeing it and learning how to lead from a superficial reading of the Gospels.

Christ redeems us from the penalty of sin, releases us from the power of sin, and shows us what it means to be a leader. Yet leaders who are devoted followers of Jesus and empowered by the Holy Spirit will continue to struggle with sin.

Leadership Struggling against Sin Today

Sin is sticky. It leaves a residue we cannot easily wipe away. No matter how much we read the Bible, pray, worship, and serve God, no matter how much faith we have or how fervent our devotion, we still have sinful desires. No matter what we do we cannot permanently rid ourselves of these embarrassing thoughts and feelings. Though we are new creatures in Christ and have been set free from slavery to sin, we continue to sin and sin sticks to us. Even becoming a leader does not lessen our temptation toward sin. Why is this?

Immediately upon conversion, God implants a new nature in every believer (2 Corinthians 5:17). This new nature frees us from slavery to sin because it is perfect and without sin (1 John 3:9). It always wants to do what is right and follow God's will. This gives us the potential to become better leaders. Though we receive a brand new nature, we keep the same old mind and body. This is our old self, also called our sinful nature or flesh (Ephesians 4:22). The flesh retains its ability to tempt us to sin. God wants us to fight against the corrupt desires of our sinful nature (Romans 8:12-13).

Sanctification is the inward, spiritual transformation of a believer and involves a life-long battle against sin. Through the Holy Spirit, God is renovating our heart and life and helping us to become better people. As God works to change our heart, we have the potential to become better leaders. But we dare not think we are trying to reform our flesh to "make it behave" so we don't sin as much. On the contrary, the Bible tells us to *cut*, *kill* and *crucify* our sinful nature (Galatians 5:24, Matthew 18:8-9). We fight against and push aside our corrupt desires and strive to live according to our new nature (Romans 8:13). Unfortunately, our flesh keeps pushing back (Galatians 5:17).

All of this pushing and fighting is too much for us if we rely only on our own strength. We cannot do it alone (Romans 7:18). Sanctification depends entirely on God's grace (Romans 8:2-4). We cannot make ourselves holy. We need the mighty inner strengthening of the Holy Spirit to accomplish this work in us (Ephesians 3:16). While we have a passive role in justification—we can do nothing to bring about our own salvation—we have an active role in sanctification (Colossians 3:9-10). Paul taught, "Throw off your old sinful nature and your former way of life, which is corrupted by lust and deception. Instead, let the Spirit renew your thoughts and attitudes. Put on your new nature, created to be like God—truly righteous and holy" (Ephesians 4:22-24). We cooperate with the Holy Spirit while remaining utterly dependent on his power. We keep on fighting the good fight of the faith (1 Timothy 6:12).

As leaders grow in grace, they become better leaders because they are putting off the flesh, clothing themselves with Christ, and getting better at not living according to their corrupt desires. As they are formed into the image of Christ, they are becoming people that others love, trust, and want to follow. But they must still daily battle against the corrupt desires of their sinful nature. Being promoted to a higher level of leadership doesn't make this process any easier. It only exposes leaders to greater power and new temptations.

As we lead others, we should not be surprised if we are tempted by gross sins. Though Christ is transforming our lives and we are becoming better people in many ways, our flesh or sinful nature remains corrupt and deceitful (Romans 7:18). Sinful desires stick to us even as we try to lead diligently and follow faithfully. Greater responsibility and authority often opens us up to fresh temptations, ones we haven't seen before. If we stumble or fall, we can take comfort that the forgiveness of Christ also covers the sins of leaders.

This is another reason why leadership doesn't work better in daily life. Leaders and followers are human beings who continue to sin. Our sinful nature gets in the way of our leading and following. Sin gums up the delicate moving parts of the leader-follower dynamic. We fall out of step with each other and we fall out of step with the Spirit (Galatians 5:25).

Every once in a while, we find ourselves on a team that really clicks or we get to follow an outstanding leader in action. By God's grace, good leadership still happens. But what we see and feel is only a grainy photocopy of what God intended when he originally created the leader-follower dynamic.

While it's obvious to us that leadership is essential here on earth, do we have any indication whether there will be any leading and following happening in heaven? Or is leadership something reserved for mortal life?

Leadership as it will be in Heaven

We can be assured that leading and following will exist in heaven because God will continue to lead his people and we will be his followers. The book of Revelation makes this plain. "I heard a loud shout from the throne, saying, 'Look, God's home is now among his people! He will live with them, and they will be his people. God himself will be with them' " (Revelation 21:3). So the Triune God will be leading his people, and his followers will live together with him.

Though we can be certain we will be following, will we actually be leading anyone else in heaven? Will we work in teams with each other or be responsible for leading other believers or possibly even angels? Heaven is outside of our ability to fully comprehend. There is no way to know for sure how leadership will work there. We can scarcely understand how leadership works here on earth. As Isaiah said, "For just as the heavens are higher than the earth, so my ways are higher than your ways and my thoughts higher than your thoughts" (Isaiah 55:9). It's wise to avoid useless speculation on such matters (Titus 3:9). We cannot know with certainty whether or not we will be leading and following each other as we follow God in heaven. But if we are leading and being led, we can be confident that it will be the kind of leading and following that God originally created, unspoiled by sin. It will be a glorified leading and following that will be far superior to the fallen leadership we experience here.

We won't have leaders who struggle against sinful desires. We won't have to worry that someone will walk up to us in heaven and point a finger saying, "You there, it's time to glorify God." We won't get stuck on a heavenly work crew with an overbearing boss who can't remember our name. The leader-follower dynamic will be without tension and friction. If we are leading each other in heaven, it will feel like pure love. We will experience perfect teamwork and synergy as we all simultaneously and joyously follow the King of kings and Lord of lords (Revelation 19:16).

That's the story of leadership from Genesis to Revelation. Leadership was God's idea. He created it to function as a wonderful leader-follower dynamic. Today leadership is fallen and leaders are incomplete people. This is why leadership doesn't work as well as we would like in daily life. One day, leadership will be restored and made perfect again.

Though we cannot know with any certainty if we will be leading others in heaven, we know for sure that we have plenty of opportunity to lead and follow well the rest of our days here on earth.

Meanwhile, Back on Earth

After the exodus from Egypt, God led the Israelites on their way by appearing to them as a pillar of cloud by day and a pillar of fire by night (Exodus 13:21). For three months he guided them in this way until he brought them to Mount Sinai. Moses went up the mountain to speak to God. "Then the Lord said to Moses, 'I will come to you in a thick cloud, Moses, so the people themselves can hear me when I speak with you. Then they will always trust you' " (Exodus 19:9). Notice that God did not say "then they will always trust *me*," but "then they will always trust *you*." God had earlier selected Moses to lead the nation, and now he was strengthening him in his position. He was reinforcing the relationship of trust that is essential for leaders and followers to be able to work together. He was fortifying Moses' position as the leader of the people. This is a significant passage demonstrating that leadership is God's idea and that he chooses to raise up and work through human leaders to accomplish his work.

God raised up many leaders in the Bible and continues to do so today. He is not sitting idly and wringing his hands hoping that some of us will step up to the challenge of leadership so that he can work through us. Rather he initiates by working in us to make us fit for leading, calling us to a life of leadership, and then placing us in particular leadership roles.

No leadership position is so high it is beyond his power or so low it is beyond his notice. Daniel understood that God "removes kings and sets up other kings" (Daniel 2:21). Daniel heard an angelic messenger proclaim, "The Most High rules over the kingdoms of the world. He gives them to anyone he chooses—even to the lowliest of people" (Daniel 4:17). Asaph wrote a psalm exclaiming, "It is God alone who judges; he decides who will rise and who will fall" (Psalm 75:7). Paul taught, "Those in positions of authority have been placed there by God" (Romans 13:1). Though these verses specifically mention kings and governments, God is not limited to dealing with leaders at the top. He is active in raising up and repositioning leaders at all levels. He strengthens some leaders (Ephesians 3:16). He also weakens others (Job 12:24). God is continually moving people in and out of leadership and accomplishing his work through them.

Knowing that God chooses to work in and through us as we lead, we should be clear that God doesn't need us. God doesn't have to rely on us, but we are wise to rely on him as we lead. Paul demonstrated the correct attitude: "After all, who is Apollos? Who is Paul? We are only God's servants through whom you believed the Good News. Each of us did the work the Lord gave us. I planted the seed in your hearts, and Apollos watered it, but it was God who made it grow. It's not important who does the planting, or who does the watering. What's important is that God makes the seed grow" (1 Corinthians 3:5-7).

God is active in the world and works through leaders, but we are often unaware when this happens. This is similar to when pastors stand up to preach. They write and rehearse their sermon, then stand in front to deliver it. Alongside of the words they speak, the Holy Spirit works in the hearts and minds of the listeners to bring them to faith and form them spiritually. The pastors are often unaware of the work God is doing through them at the moment. The same is true for teachers. They study their lesson and stand before a Bible class or sit with a small group and get their students thinking deeply about a Bible passage. Again the Holy Spirit works in the hearts and minds of the learners to help them understand the meaning of Scripture and apply it to life. The teachers may or may not sense God at work in the discussion. God works through leaders in a similar way. We enlist followers, make plans, show individual concern, give direction, inspire, monitor progress, and evaluate. Whether we are aware of it or not, the Holy Spirit is using our words and actions to shape lives and accomplish God's will. God works through leaders, but he often hides himself while doing so (Isaiah 45:15).

Two Sides of the Same Coin

When we begin to view leadership as a part of the leadership-followership dynamic, we can better understand that leadership and followership are two sides of the same coin. It is a serious mistake to view these as separate and different.

Leadership is not a position, a personality type, or a set of behaviors. Leadership is an interaction between a leader and followers. It involves a relationship between leaders and followers. A good question to ask is this: if someone 'leads' and nobody follows, did leadership actually occur?

So when we approach the Bible for insights on leadership, we would be wise to also look for insights on followership. In fact, one cannot become a good leader without first becoming a good follower.

Biblical Leadership

People who want to make sure they are leading in a God-pleasing way turn to the Bible to look for guidance. Books, articles, and

Bible studies about leadership tend to use three main approaches for identifying Biblical principles.

Direct teaching: This approach involves compiling Bible passages that teach us how to lead. Relevant verses include handling authority, guidelines for elders, and advice to kings. For example, Jesus said, "You know that the rulers in this world lord it over their people, and officials flaunt their authority over those under them. But among you it will be different. Whoever wants to be a leader among you must be your servant" (Matthew 20:25-26).

Examples of leaders: This approach examines leaders in the Bible—both good and bad—and sifts principles we can apply as we lead. One of the most popular leaders to study for leadership principles is Nehemiah.

Jesus as the perfect leader: This approach focuses on Jesus as the greatest leader in history. He is the only perfect leader because he was the only perfect person who has ever lived. If we are to become like Jesus in all ways (2 Corinthians 3:18), then it would only make sense that we should lead like him as well.

But what if we were to look at this from another angle? Instead of focusing narrowly on leadership, what if we looked at what the Bible teaches about leadership and followership? Instead of looking only at what the leader is doing, what if we look at the interaction of leaders and followers in the Bible?

The Bible has a lot to teach us about following well. This means we would have a lot more Biblical material to work with. In fact, for every Bible verse relating to leadership, there are at least ten relating to following well. Biblical teaching about followership could bring us fresh insights into leadership.

Biblical Followership

One can make the argument that the Bible is not meant to be a leadership handbook. But it can certainly be considered a handbook for followers. Not everybody is called to be a leader, but God wants all of his children to follow well.

To discover Biblical principles of followership, we can use the same three approaches.

Direct teaching: This involves compiling Bible passages that teach people how to follow well. For example, we are to obey our leaders (Hebrews 13:17). We are to submit to all governmental authorities (1 Peter 2:13). In addition, every verse that tells us how to treat other people applies to those who want to follow well because leaders are people, too. We cannot claim our leader is not also our neighbor (Luke 10:29).

Examples of followers: We can study examples of followers in the Bible—both good and bad followers—for principles to apply. Every individual mentioned in the Bible was a follower of God and of other people. Some followed well and others were rebellious or disobedient. Ruth is an outstanding example of someone who followed well.

Jesus as the perfect follower: Jesus is the only person who has lived who has followed our Heavenly Father perfectly. He is the best example to imitate for anyone who wants to be a follower of God.

If we study the Bible, carefully paying attention to both sides of the leader-follower dynamic, then we can become better followers and better leaders simultaneously. Every book in the Bible offers insight into following well.

Why Everyone Should Care about Becoming a Better Follower

Some might say, "I don't care about following well. I want to lead. I want others to follow me well." Or, "I already know how to follow—been there, done that—I want to improve my leadership now." Here are some reasons why everyone should care about following well and continuing to grow as a follower throughout life.

First, the best followers are more likely to be the best leaders. Those who have followed well know what kind of behavior and attitudes they want to develop in the people they lead. Those who don't know how to develop their followers take a shortcut and simply demand results. Whenever somebody is engaged in leadership, he or she is leading followers. The more we understand about following, the better we will be at leading followers. Those best at following well are the ones most able to show others how to follow well.

Second, being a good follower helps us to deal with poor leaders. A courageous follower is not afraid to pull leaders aside and give them straightforward feedback on how to lead better. He or she will be able to tell incompetent leaders what people need in order to be led well. Good followers help leaders lead.

Third, all of us will always remain a follower. No matter what leadership position we attain in life or how high we climb on the ladder of leadership, we will always be following somebody. If someone becomes a supervisor, she follows the lead of a manager.

If she becomes a manager, she reports to an executive. Even if she becomes the CEO of a large company she will be accountable to the owner or a board of directors who set targets for performance. Even if she is totally in charge at a business she owns, in other areas of life she will still be following others. Because we will remain a follower the rest of our life, we might as well learn to follow well.

Fourth, how well we follow others offers people quick insight into our character. If someone cannot take direction or avoids accountability, others will spot that shortcoming instantly. When someone is rebellious or indignant under the direction of others, character flaws show through like warning lights. A leader can be haughty and people may not see it clearly. But when a follower is haughty the lack of humility is plain for all to see. Poor followers cannot use the excuse that they are "natural leaders" or "alpha males" by instinct. They simply have a glaring weakness that is problematic. Poor followership reveals poor character.

Three Types of Followership

Both the Old and New Testaments are filled with passages containing direct teaching about followership. Both contain inspiring stories about people who followed well. When trying to understand what the Bible teaches about following well, we must first answer a foundational question: Who are we following?

The Bible talks about what it means to follow well in three distinct contexts. Let's call these types of followership Type I, Type II, and Type III. Type I is following God. Type II is following an inherited authority. Type III is following another human being. In each type an individual is following a different kind of leader. This is an important distinction because if we get the Biblical teaching confused among these three contexts, then follower abuse is more likely to occur.

Type I followership means following God. Before Jesus ascended to Heaven, he commanded that believers make disciples of all nations. A disciple is a follower of Jesus. Following Jesus requires faith, which comes from God. Though some of the following we do will one day come to an end, Type I followership is eternal. We will always remain a follower of Jesus. Even in heaven we will still be following him. Following God demands giving our whole self to him. This is the most demanding of the three types of followership. Jesus taught that we should love God with all of our heart, soul, and mind (Matthew 22:37). That's means giving it all we've got.

Type I followership is strict. We are commanded to love God. We are commanded to love our neighbor as our self (Matthew 22:39). We are commanded to make disciples (Matthew 28:18-20). We are commanded to love one another (2 John 1:5). These are not merely divine suggestions or helpful hints for a more fulfilling life. Fortunately, God's commands are not burdensome (1 John 5:2-3).

Type I followership involves suffering. Jesus said he expected each of his followers to take up their cross and follow him (Matthew 16:24). He added that anyone who does not carry his or her cross cannot be his disciple (Luke 14:27). But he comforts us by letting us know his yoke is easy and his burden is light (Matthew 11:30).

In Type I leadership, we are never following other people such as a pastor or a Bible teacher. Instead, our spiritual leaders are shepherds, guides, encouragers, and examples that help us follow Christ better. Type I followership necessitates that every believer have a direct, personal connection to Jesus. There are no layers of management in Type I followership. When pastors and teachers and evangelists are ministering faithfully, they are standing alongside and helping others become better followers of Jesus. If they are faithfully shepherding the flock, they can never insert themselves between the Good Shepherd and the sheep.

God can use spiritual leaders in a powerful way as they teach us about God's grace and as they live lives worth imitating (1 Corinthians 11:1). We dare not take their spiritual authority lightly. When a servant of God who is called by God is teaching the truth of God, the people of God should obey. Hebrews 13:17 says, "Obey your spiritual leaders, and do what they say. Their work is to watch over your souls, and they are accountable to God. Give them reason to do this with joy and not with sorrow. That would certainly not be for your benefit." This is Type I followership. But when that same human being is serving in a role as leader in any organizational setting such as a church or nonprofit ministry, then leading and following falls into the realm of Type III followership.

A comforting insight for us here is that there is no possibility for follower abuse in Type I followership. God is never incompetent, uncaring, unfeeling, or manipulative. We may face persecution in this world, but that comes from the hands of other people and not from God. We will certainly experience suffering. We may be punished for doing wrong, but that's simply justice not follower abuse. We may experience distress for foolish decisions, but that's living with the consequences of our actions, not follower abuse. The ultimate follower abuse emanates from the Evil One. Those who get involved in the occult and willingly follow Satan are signing up for horrifying follower abuse in this life and the next.

Type I followership is the source for developing a servant's heart that is crucial for good leadership. As we grow in faith and Christ is formed in us, we develop a greater capacity to serve others because we do so for the sake of Christ, not for what we get out of it. As we become more like Christ, we grow in our ability to empty ourselves just as Christ did when he came to earth as a man, made himself nothing, and became a servant (Philippians 2:5-7).

Caleb was someone who was affirmed and rewarded for following well. He was one of the twelve men sent ahead to spy on the people living in the Promised Land and one of the two who encouraged the people to obey God and take the land. After the people rebelled, all of the adults were sentenced to die in the wilderness. During that incident God added, "But because my servant Caleb has a different spirit and follows me wholeheartedly, I will bring him into the land he went to, and his descendants will inherit it" (Numbers 14:24). This story of Caleb is a just one example of Type I followership. The Bible is filled with examples of people who follow God well.

Selected Passages Related to Type I Followership

My sheep listen to my voice; I know them, and they follow me. John 10:27

Jesus called out to them, "Come, follow me, and I will show you how to fish for people!" Matthew 4:19

Then Jesus said to his disciples, "If any of you wants to be my follower, you must turn from your selfish ways, take up your cross, and follow me." Matthew 16:24

And if you do not carry your own cross and follow me, you cannot be my disciple. Luke 14:27

We know we love God's children if we love God and obey his commandments. Loving God means keeping his commandments, and his commandments are not burdensome. 1 John 5:2-3

*Serve only the Lord your God and fear him alone.
Obey his commands, listen to his voice, and cling to
him.* Deuteronomy 13:4

*But be very careful to obey all the commands and the
instructions that Moses gave to you. Love the Lord
your God, walk in all his ways, obey his commands,
hold firmly to him, and serve him with all your heart
and all your soul.* Joshua 22:5

*"I am the Lord your God," I told them. "Follow my
decrees, pay attention to my regulations."* Ezekiel
20:19

*Jesus told them, "This is the only work God wants from
you: Believe in the one he has sent."* John 6:29

And you should imitate me, just as I imitate Christ.
1 Corinthians 11:1

*May God, who gives this patience and encouragement,
help you live in complete harmony with each other, as
is fitting for followers of Christ Jesus.* Romans 15:5

*Remember your leaders who taught you the word of
God. Think of all the good that has come from their
lives, and follow the example of their faith.* Hebrews
13:7

Type II followership means following an inherited authority.
When we are born, we automatically become a part of a family
and a state. We don't have the option of choosing our parents or
our government. We inherit them. As children, we grow up under

parental authority. As adults, we live and work under governmental authority. Our role is to obey family rules and civil law. We are to honor both our parents (Ephesians 6:1) and our governmental leaders (Romans 13:7).

The Bible speaks clearly and plainly that when we are born again and become citizens of God's kingdom, we remain citizens here on this earth and under the authority of the government where we reside. In this way, all believers have a dual citizenship. No one can act as if the government no longer applies to him because he has suddenly become a citizen of the Kingdom of God.

In Type II followership, we respect and follow leaders when they are carrying out the duties of their office. But when they are no longer in office, whether appointed or elected, they no longer have the same authority over us. Some governmental leaders get used to the power of their office and try to retain their power and prestige even when their term expires. But we don't have to obey them when they're no longer in office. Their authority is contained in their official position, not in their person.

We also don't have to obey them when they overextend the power of their position or overreach their authority. We can refuse to obey them when they ask us to do something that goes against Scripture or is clearly unethical or against the law of the land. Type I followership trumps Type II followership when the two are in conflict.

Type II followership applies to all levels of government. Some people think they're doing well by obeying federal laws while ignoring lesser laws such as city or village ordinances. Or speed limits. These Biblical teachings apply to all levels of government from federal legislation to community ordinances. So we should strive to follow well in Type II followership even as it applies to paying a parking ticket, obtaining a fishing license, or securing a building permit for a remodeling project.

In Type II followership, we are not required to love the government with all our heart and soul and mind and strength. We are simply to be good citizens, pray for our leaders, and give honor to whoever honor is due.

Type II followership works similarly in a family. Parents make rules that children are to obey. Some parents are stricter than others. That doesn't matter. Some nations are more restrictive than others, too. Just as God has established nations and governments, he established families and parents.

The Ten Commandments state that we are to honor our father and mother (Exodus 20:12). This command does not expire when we move out of the house. Though we become adults and take responsibility for our own lives, we still have the obligation to honor our father and mother and care for them in their old age. As we become independent and responsible for ourselves and live on our own, we no longer have to obey our parents. Becoming independent is an important part of becoming an adult. But our obligation to honor our father and mother continues.

Most of us deeply love our parents, but our love for God should be deeper still. Jesus said that if anyone comes to him and does not "hate" his father and mother in comparison, then that person is not worthy to be his disciple (Luke 14:26). Type I followership is markedly different than Type II.

The family and the state have been created by God for our protection and well-being. We inherit them and pass them on to our children and the next generation of citizens.

Selected Passages Related to Type II Followership

Honor your father and mother. Then you will live a long, full life in the land the Lord your God is giving you. Exodus 20:12

Each of you must show great respect for your mother and father, and you must always observe my Sabbath days of rest. I am the Lord your God. Leviticus 19:3

My son, obey your father's commands, and don't neglect your mother's instruction. Proverbs 6:20

Children, obey your parents because you belong to the Lord, for this is the right thing to do. "Honor your father and mother." This is the first commandment with a promise: If you honor your father and mother, "things will go well for you, and you will have a long life on the earth." Ephesians 6:1-3

Children, always obey your parents, for this pleases the Lord. Colossians 3:20

Everyone must submit to governing authorities. For all authority comes from God, and those in positions of authority have been placed there by God. Romans 13:1

For the Lord's sake, respect all human authority— whether the king as head of state, or the officials he has appointed. For the king has sent them to punish those who do wrong and to honor those who do right. 1 Peter 2:13-14

Pay your taxes, too, for these same reasons. For government workers need to be paid. They are serving God in what they do. Romans 13:6

Give to everyone what you owe them: Pay your taxes and government fees to those who collect them, and give respect and honor to those who are in authority. Romans 13:7

I urge you, first of all, to pray for all people. Ask God to help them; intercede on their behalf, and give thanks for them. Pray this way for kings and all who are in authority so that we can live peaceful and quiet lives marked by godliness and dignity. 1 Timothy 2:1-2

Respect everyone, and love your Christian brothers and sisters. Fear God, and respect the king. 1 Peter 2:17

Type III followership means following other human beings. If Type I is following God and Type II is following inherited authorities which have been established by God, then Type III followership is following another human being in any other context. Type III followership is following the lead of another person at work, church, on a team, in a group, volunteer organization, or other social setting. Type III followership differs considerably from the other two types.

Type III followership involves following leaders with and without organizational authority. A manager at work may have a high level of organizational authority with the ability to hire and fire, give raises and withhold perks. A coordinator of volunteers at a nonprofit organization, on the other hand, may have a medium or low level of authority depending on the organizational culture. Someone passionate for a worthwhile cause and wanting to mobilize others has no authority so must rely on personal ability to persuade. These all fall into the category of Type III followership.

The Bible has lot to say about Type III followership because the leader is a human being created in the image of God. As a follower, you have a relationship with that leader at some level. This means that every verse in the Bible that tells us how to treat another individual applies to our relationships with our leaders.

The logic here is deceptively simple. We are to treat leaders with love just like any human being. We do not have license to treat them with less courtesy or respect or patience because they are serving in a leadership role. Yet it is so easy for followers to criticize those who lead them. It's easy to view them as problems, enemies, or objects.

Following another person is a free choice. We can choose to continue following any individual or choose to follow someone else. This includes working for an employer. We are free to follow well at work and we are free to leave that place of employment and get a different job. We are not free to follow poorly. If we do so we will violate the principles of Type III followership.

Paul taught that we are to submit ourselves to the governing authorities (Romans 13:1). He did not say that we are to submit ourselves to the boss at work in the same way simply because we receive a paycheck from the company. That would be misapplying Type II followership in a Type III context.

As children we were continually told to obey our parents. What was being impressed upon us was simply compliance. When we get older, if we haven't given the subject much thought, we can carry this infantile view of authority into the workplace and mistakenly think we should obey our immediate supervisor in the same way. When studying the Bible, we read that we are to obey every authority

(1 Peter 2:13), meaning governmental, and we can easily assume that every authority includes our place of employment. Some bosses would have us believe that. We don't have to have the same degree of loyalty to our employer as we should reserve for Jesus. We don't have to submit to our boss as we do for someone with governmental authority. Type III followership is fully negotiable. If the other party isn't living up to their end of the deal, we are free to go somewhere else. We are free to follow a different leader.

Pastors and Bible teachers represent a special case. They have a dual role as they carry both spiritual authority and organizational authority. As followers, we should be careful about confusing the two. One example would be a pastor who is losing an argument or not getting his way on something and says, "I'm the pastor! You have to listen to me on this." Spiritual leaders should never misuse spiritual authority.

Paul urged the believers in Thessalonica to follow well in their congregation. "Dear brothers and sisters, honor those who are your leaders in the Lord's work. They work hard among you and give you spiritual guidance. Show them great respect and wholehearted love because of their work. And live peacefully with each other" (1 Thessalonians 5:12-13).

Pastors are people called to an official position of ministry. Inasmuch as they are teaching or preaching the Bible and what God commands, we should listen carefully to what they say and obey. Their posture should be as people coming alongside us teaching us about how to be a better Type I follower. We should listen to them as individuals speaking the words of God to us.

But when they are in a board meeting, staff meeting, or committee meeting discussing a budget item or program issue, they are human beings in an organizational leadership role, and Type III followership applies. The apostle Peter instructed shepherds of God's flock to avoid abusive leadership. "Don't lord it over the people assigned to your care, but lead them by your own good example (1 Peter 5:3). Recognizing that Type III followership applies, we must still focus on following our spiritual leaders well (Hebrews 13:17).

This can be confusing, but in any given interaction the pastor is either talking to us as one of the sheep in God's flock or as one of the volunteers serving in a ministry of the congregation. People can easily confuse Type I and Type III followership when following a spiritual leader. This is one reason why follower abuse occurs in local churches, too.

So no matter who we are following, whether a supervisor at work, a team leader at church, or a paid staff person at a volunteer event, all Biblical principles about how to treat other people apply. We should treat our human leaders with respect (1 Peter 2:17). We should pray for them (James 5:16). We should remain humble to the point of considering others as better than ourselves (Philippians 2:3). We should show kindness and goodness to them (Galatians 5:22). We should not hate any leaders in our heart (Leviticus 19:17). We should try to live at peace with all leaders as much as possible (Romans 12:18).

Following well in any organizational context means establishing a relationship with the leader, clarifying our roles and responsibilities, taking initiative, and doing more than is asked of us. It involves giving feedback to the leader, assisting the leader, and helping the leader to lead well. All of this is simply fulfilling our part in the leader-follower dynamic.

We are free to follow another human being well and free to choose not to follow and leave. We are not free to follow selectively, picking and choosing what we will do or when we will cooperate. That is what poor followers do. If we don't want to follow someone, we can ask for a transfer, find another job, or join another congregation where we will be able to follow well. Following poorly in any organizational or social context is not an option. Fools follow poorly. Selfish people follow poorly. Those with character flaws follow poorly.

Selected Passages Related to Type III Followership

Do not seek revenge or bear a grudge against a fellow Israelite, but love your neighbor as yourself. I am the Lord. Leviticus 19:18

Forgive us our sins, as we have forgiven those who sin against us. Matthew 6:12

Do all that you can to live in peace with everyone. Romans 12:18

Do to others whatever you would like them to do to you. This is the essence of all that is taught in the law and the prophets. Matthew 7:12

If another believer sins against you, go privately and point out the offense. If the other person listens and confesses it, you have won that person back. Matthew 18:15

But to you who are willing to listen, I say, love your enemies! Do good to those who hate you. Bless those who curse you. Pray for those who hurt you. Luke 6:27-28

You must be compassionate, just as your Father is compassionate. Luke 6:36

So watch yourselves! If another believer sins, rebuke that person; then if there is repentance, forgive. Luke 17:3

Love each other with genuine affection, and take delight in honoring each other. Romans 12:10

When God's people are in need, be ready to help them. Always be eager to practice hospitality. Romans 12:13

Never pay back evil with more evil. Do things in such a way that everyone can see you are honorable. Romans 12:17

Dear friends, never take revenge. Leave that to the righteous anger of God. For the Scriptures say, "I will take revenge; I will pay them back," says the Lord. Romans 12:19

Owe nothing to anyone—except for your obligation to love one another. If you love your neighbor, you will fulfill the requirements of God's law. Romans 13:8

So then, let us aim for harmony in the church and try to build each other up. Romans 14:19

We should help others do what is right and build them up in the Lord. Romans 15:2

We work wearily with our own hands to earn our living. We bless those who curse us. We are patient with those who abuse us. 1 Corinthians 4:12

And do everything with love. 1 Corinthians 16:14

We are careful to be honorable before the Lord, but we also want everyone else to see that we are honorable.
2 Corinthians 8:21

For you have been called to live in freedom, my brothers and sisters. But don't use your freedom to satisfy your sinful nature. Instead, use your freedom to serve one another in love. For the whole law can be summed up in this one command: "Love your neighbor as yourself." Galatians 5:13-14

Dear brothers and sisters, if another believer is overcome by some sin, you who are godly should gently and humbly help that person back onto the right path. And be careful not to fall into the same temptation yourself. Galatians 6:1

So let's not get tired of doing what is good. At just the right time we will reap a harvest of blessing if we don't give up. Therefore, whenever we have the opportunity, we should do good to everyone—especially to those in the family of faith. Galatians 6:9-10

Always be humble and gentle. Be patient with each other, making allowance for each other's faults because of your love. Ephesians 4:2

So stop telling lies. Let us tell our neighbors the truth, for we are all parts of the same body. Ephesians 4:25

Don't use foul or abusive language. Let everything you say be good and helpful, so that your words will be an encouragement to those who hear them. Ephesians 4:29

Instead, be kind to each other, tenderhearted, forgiving one another, just as God through Christ has forgiven you. Ephesians 4:32

Make allowance for each other's faults, and forgive anyone who offends you. Remember, the Lord forgave you, so you must forgive others. Colossians 3:13

So encourage each other and build each other up, just as you are already doing. 1 Thessalonians 5:11

Brothers and sisters, we urge you to warn those who are lazy. Encourage those who are timid. Take tender care of those who are weak. Be patient with everyone. 1 Thessalonians 5:14

See that no one pays back evil for evil, but always try to do good to each other and to all people. 1 Thessalonians 5:15

Let us think of ways to motivate one another to acts of love and good works. Hebrews 10:24

Work at living in peace with everyone, and work at living a holy life, for those who are not holy will not see the Lord. Hebrews 12:14

And don't forget to do good and to share with those in need. These are the sacrifices that please God. Hebrews 13:16

Yes indeed, it is good when you obey the royal law as found in the Scriptures: "Love your neighbor as yourself." James 2:8

> *Finally, all of you should be of one mind. Sympathize with each other. Love each other as brothers and sisters. Be tenderhearted, and keep a humble attitude.* 1 Peter 3:8

> *Don't repay evil for evil. Don't retaliate with insults when people insult you. Instead, pay them back with a blessing. That is what God has called you to do, and he will bless you for it.* 1 Peter 3:9

> *Most important of all, continue to show deep love for each other, for love covers a multitude of sins.* 1 Peter 4:8

We can find all three types of followership in a single verse in 1 Peter 2:17: "Respect everyone, and love your Christian brothers and sisters. Fear God, and respect the king."

The goal of Type I followership is total obedience. The goal of Type II is full compliance. The goal of Type III is to create the conditions for the leader-follower dynamic to occur.

Type I followership is impossible apart from God's grace and the work of the Holy Spirit in our lives. Type II is mandatory. It's the law! Type III is voluntary. It's negotiable. We are free to choose. We are free to help it happen.

Type I	Type II		Type III	
Following God	Following Inherited Authorities		Following Human Beings	
Spiritual Authority	Parental Authority	Legal Authority	With organizational authority	Without organizational authority
Covenant	House rules and civil law		Contracts, agreements, expectations, relationships	
Unable to follow	Forced to follow		Free to follow	
Obedience empowered by the Holy Spirit	Obedience is mandatory		Obedience is voluntary	
Follower abuse is impossible because God loves us	Follower abuse is common because power corrupts		Follower abuse happens when leaders view people as objects	
Eternal	Lifetime		Temporary	

Five Levels of Followership

When we look at how well people follow, it's evident that some are good followers, others are only fair followers, and many are poor followers. When we look at our own performance as a follower in several areas of life, we will see places where we are following well and other areas where we are not. To bring more clarity to what it means to follow well, it is useful to divide followership into five levels with those following well on the top and those following poorly on the bottom.

Jesus told a parable about ten servants where some of them followed well and some of them followed poorly (Luke 19:12-27). A nobleman was going away to be crowned king and gave ten of his servants one mina each. When he returned, he called the servants together to see how much profit that they had earned for him. One servant invested the money and earned ten more minas (level five). Another invested the money and earned five more (level four). But one servant followed poorly and hid the money away doing nothing to earn more for his master. For this investment strategy he was called a wicked servant (level two). The least he could have done was to deposit the money to earn interest on it (level three). Then the king ordered that his enemies (level one) be rounded up and killed.

Level of Followership	Parable of the Ten Servants in Luke 19	Leader-Follower Dynamic
5	First servant invested the mina and earned 10 more (v.16)	Someone who is following well, helping other followers, helping the leader lead, sense of oneness with the leader
4	Second servant invested the mina and earned 5 more (v.18)	Someone who is following well, helping other followers, and supportive of the leader, sense of teamwork with the leader
3	Any servant could have deposited the money to earn interest on it (v.23)	Someone who is doing the minimum required, mere compliance, a sheep, sense of following the leader
2	Third servant returned the mina after hiding it (v.20)	Someone who is not fulfilling responsibilities, falling behind, a slacker, sense of distance from the leader
1	Enemies were rounded up to be killed (v. 27)	Someone who is undercutting or resisting, making things worse, sense of antagonism toward the leader

These five levels of followership we see in this parable can help followers raise their performance to a higher level. It is also useful for leaders to know what followers need from them at each level.

Level Five Followers. These are the most mature and engaged of all followers. They not only fulfill their role completely, they also help others follow well and help the leader to lead. They are willing to stand up to a leader who is not doing what is right or best for everyone. They look for ways to help the leader-follower dynamic to work better. They may also take the lead in short bursts if they have special expertise in an area. What level five followers need from a leader is simply time and opportunities.

Level Four Followers. These followers are also fully engaged in the group or team and committed to the goal. They fulfill their role completely but also look for ways to encourage and assist others. They are concerned for everybody in the group and will do things to improve team spirit. What level four followers need from leaders is goals and resources.

Level Three Followers. These followers are the ones that basically do their job without complaint. Their concern is usually limited to their role and getting their work done. They are usually unconcerned about making the work of leading easier for the leader. What level three followers need from leaders is direction and support.

Level Two Followers. These followers are somewhat disengaged and either can't or won't fulfill their duties up to what is expected. Sometimes they need help from others to do their work. They never do more than they are asked. They do not look for ways to help other team members. What level two followers need from leaders is encouragement and assistance.

Level One Followers. These followers are the ones that make leadership difficult. They are disruptive, defensive, and block the work of the leader. They are resistant to the leader and usually not committed to the goals of the group. These are the most difficult followers to deal with. Leaders need to find ways to neutralize any bad affects they are having on team performance or on the motivation of other followers. What level one followers need from leaders is direct feedback.

Anyone can spot all five levels of followership on display at a typical youth group meeting. Courageous followers are the students who are working closely with the adult leaders and inviting their friends from school. The engaged followers have their Bibles open, participate in discussion, ask questions, and have fun with others afterwards. The compliant followers will be sitting quietly, listening, and following along. They might join in the discussion once in a while. We spot the disengaged followers texting on their cell phone or talking to their friends in their clique. They are oblivious to what is happening in room. We will see some disruptive followers teasing each other, drawing attention away from the leaders, and generally making it difficult to conduct the Bible study portion of the meeting.

We all have roles in life where we are following a leader. In general, we should be following at level four or five in every area of life. Consider how the parable of the Minas ends. To the level five follower the king said, "You are a good servant. You have been faithful with the little I entrusted to you, so you will be governor of ten cities as your reward" (Luke 19:17). Then he entrusted five cities to the level four follower. The king exclaimed "Well done!" to both of them. The top two levels of followership are divinely blessed with increasing levels of trust, opportunity, responsibility, and authority.

We can see many similarities of each level of followership across the three types of followership.

Five Levels of Type I Followership. Type I followership is following God. At the highest level we would expect to see wholehearted disciples who are seeing more of the sin in their heart, growing in their appreciation of God's grace toward them, trusting in Christ more fully for their righteousness, and living with their faith expressing itself through love (Galatians 5:6). At level four we would have growing disciples who are responding to the work of the Holy Spirit in their heart. They engage in growth enhancing activities such as reading or listening to the Bible regularly, praying with expectancy, worshiping God joyfully, and connecting with others through a small group or service team. At level three we would have nominal disciples who may attend church regularly but who are not growing in their faith or love for God and others. They will identify themselves as Christians but might give little thought about God during the week. They own a Bible but do not study it. At level two we have disciples who have become distracted by the cares of this world, the deceitfulness of wealth, and other desires (Mark 4:19). Their life is too busy to take time to worship, pray, or read the Bible. They are believers but they do not worship regularly and do not engage in personal spiritual disciplines. At the lowest level, we would have wayward disciples who have given up on following God or shipwrecked their faith (1 Timothy 1:19). They may have become ensnared in sin or fallen away from God's grace (Galatians 5:4).

If we want to follow God well, then we would want to follow at level four or five.

Five Levels of Type II Followership. Type II followership is following inherited authorities. For children this means obeying parents and for adults it means being good citizens. At level five, we would have exemplary citizens who are actively involved in some way. These are people who not only follow all the laws, but work to make the laws better. They will be working to create better neighborhoods, communities, schools, and government. These are activist citizens.

At level four, we would have concerned citizens who are not only obeying the laws but are also supporting activists and voting for trustworthy political leaders. At level three we would have law-abiding citizens who comply with all laws and don't cheat on their taxes. They are doing nothing wrong but they are also not involved in making their neighborhood, city, or state a better place to live. At level two, we would see apathetic citizens who don't vote, don't care about the government, and may disregard laws if they feel they won't get caught. At the lowest level, we would have lawless citizens who are only concerned for themselves and violate the rights of others.

If we want to be good citizens, then we would want to follow at level four or five.

Five Levels of Type III Followership. Type III followership is following another human being whether as an employee at work, a volunteer at a nonprofit, or allowing ourselves be influenced by a leader in any other social context. Level five ought to reflect the leader-follower dynamic that God intended when he created it. So we would expect to see followers who are working so synergistically with their leader that one can hardly tell who is leading and who is following. These are courageous followers who are following well, encouraging other followers, and helping the leader lead well. They fulfill their roles and look ahead to anticipate problems and spot new opportunities. They will confront the leader if he or she is going the wrong way. They are fully engaged and fully supportive of the leader. At level four we would see engaged followers who are fulfilling their responsibilities, working well with other followers, and doing what they can to be a part of a high-performing team. They are energetically doing more than required. At level three, we would see followers who pay attention, strive for quality work, and follow all procedures.

They try to work well with others. They are basically doing their job. No one can fault them. At level two, we would see followers who are disengaged at work or in their volunteer role. They do not give their best effort but only enough to get by. They are passive and wait to be told what to do. Often they are lethargic. They may be physically present but their mind is somewhere else. At the lowest level, we have disruptive followers who complain, argue, and block progress of the team. They are not aligned with the goals of the leader. They make decisions for self-benefit at the expense of team members and the organization.

If we want to follow well as an employee, student, volunteer, or group member, then we would want to follow at level four or five.

Level of Engagement	Type I Followership	Type II Followership	Type III Followership
5	Wholehearted disciple	Activist citizen	Courageous follower
4	Growing disciple	Concerned citizen	Engaged follower
3	Nominal disciple	Law-abiding citizen	Compliant follower
2	Distracted disciple	Apathetic citizen	Disengaged follower
1	Wayward disciple	Lawless citizen	Disruptive follower

The point of the levels is that if we want to be good followers, then we will want to follow at level four or five in every aspect of life. We can take an inventory of every role where we are leading or following a leader and rate ourselves on this followership scale. If we are not following God well, we should pray that the Lord would help us grow spiritually. We might ask for some help to get unstuck and growing again. We might find a friend or an accountability group.

If we tend not to vote in elections, we can educate ourselves about candidates or find a cause we can enthusiastically endorse. Unlike the first two types, Type III followership is negotiable. If we can't follow a nonprofit leader well, we can find another role or leave and volunteer in another organization. The workplace is similar. If we can't follow a manager well at work, we can ask for a transfer or look for another job. If we can't find a different job, then we can simply work at following better where we are. We can grow where we are planted.

If we find ourselves at a low level of followership in any area of life, we should remember that we cannot blame our level of followership on the leader or the organization. We alone are responsible for our own actions and reactions. We are free to be a courageous follower no matter how incompetent of a leader we serve under. The goal of effective people is to follow at level four or five in every area of life.

What's wrong with level three? Those following at this level are compliant. They aren't causing problems. This is following, but it is not following well. This is the level of sheep. They are doing what they are told, following the rules, not causing problems, and fulfilling their duties, but following well involves more. Following well means helping other followers and striving for synergy with the leader. Following well means doing your part to create a high-performing team. It means taking initiative. Following well means being fully engaged in the job or volunteer role. Level three is generic, plain vanilla, mere following. Levels four and five are following well. It was the servants in the parable who performed at levels four and five who both earned the praise of the king, "Well done!" (Luke 19:17, 19). This parable teaches us that following well is divinely blessed and will be rewarded.

The Bible holds stories of many people who followed well. Joseph went above and beyond when serving under Potiphar and the

Pharaoh of Egypt (Genesis 41:33-36). Caleb stood up against the other spies and encouraged the people to take the land (Numbers 13:30). Ruth followed Naomi. Jonathan committed himself to the leadership of David. Shadrach, Meshach, and Abednego followed Daniel. The leaders in Jerusalem courageously followed Nehemiah to rebuild the walls. The disciples followed Jesus. Timothy followed Paul. We have much to learn from their examples.

The Bible also has strong warnings for those who are not following well. Paul said to do everything without complaining or arguing (Philippines 2:14). He also taught that we should not act selfishly (Philippians 2:3). Peter said we should rid ourselves of any deceit, hypocrisy, or unkind speech (1 Peter 2:1). Level four and five followers will do their best to help followers who've become disruptive. Even well-intentioned followers can sometimes become disruptive.

If you want to be a leader with the full blessing of God, learn what it means to follow well in all areas of your life.

Becoming a REAL Follower

The Bible contains direct teaching on following well and provides hundreds of examples of both good and bad followers. Every book in the Bible offers helpful guidance about followership. If we used a computer to print out every relevant passage and sorted them into piles, we could group the passages into categories that would describe the major characteristics of good followers. There are many ways to group these passages into categories. One way to sum up the passages into four categories that are memorable is REAL: Responsible, Ethical, Authentic, and Loving. Those who want to follow well need to get REAL.

Responsible. People who follow well take responsibility. They are self-disciplined, willing to be accountable, and they fulfill their duties faithfully. Responsible followers are alert and take ownership. They take initiative. They do what they say they are going to do. They are concerned about the effectiveness and quality of what they produce. They are disciplined in setting clear boundaries for people yet take notice of how others are doing and stand ready to help out when needed. They are not lazy, irresponsible, or uncaring, and are not characterized as slackers in any way. They don't look the other way when things go wrong or back away from their duties.

Joseph is an excellent example of what it means to be a responsible follower. After Joseph was sold into slavery by his brothers, he had little reason to do more than the bare minimum for his Egyptian master. But Joseph was a responsible person. So he did what he was told to do and he did it well. The master gave Joseph more to do, and he did that well. The Lord blessed Joseph with success. The Egyptian master put him in charge of his whole house, and then everything he had in the house and in the field. Joseph didn't complain or neglect any of his duties. He was a responsible follower. More than two years later he was pulled out of the dungeon to interpret a dream for Pharaoh. Immediately after telling Pharaoh the meaning of his dream, he immediately offered a plan to store up grain and save the people (Genesis 41:33-34). Nobody asked Joseph for a plan. Because he was a responsible person, Pharaoh put Joseph in charge of the new famine relief program.

Selected Passages related to being Responsible

So be on your guard, not asleep like the others. Stay alert and be clearheaded. 1 Thessalonians 5:6

Stay alert! Watch out for your great enemy, the devil. He prowls around like a roaring lion, looking for someone to devour. 1 Peter 5:8

For God has not given us a spirit of fear and timidity, but of power, love, and self-discipline. 2 Timothy 1:7

So be careful how you live. Don't live like fools, but like those who are wise. Ephesians 5:15

Don't look out only for your own interests, but take an interest in others, too. Philippians 2:4

God has given each of you a gift from his great variety of spiritual gifts. Use them well to serve one another. 1 Peter 4:10

Work with enthusiasm, as though you were working for the Lord rather than for people. Ephesians 6:7

If another believer sins against you, go privately and point out the offense. If the other person listens and confesses it, you have won that person back. But if you are unsuccessful, take one or two others with you and go back again, so that everything you say may be confirmed by two or three witnesses. Matthew 18:15-16

Dear brothers and sisters, if another believer is overcome by some sin, you who are godly should gently and humbly help that person back onto the right path. And be careful not to fall into the same temptation yourself. Share each other's burdens, and in this way obey the law of Christ. Galatians 6:1-2

*Since this new way gives us such confidence, we can be
very bold.* 2 Corinthians 3:12

*Be on guard. Stand firm in the faith. Be courageous.
Be strong.* 1 Corinthians 16:13

*Now, a person who is put in charge as a manager must
be faithful.* 1 Corinthians 4:2

Ethical. Those who follow well are ethical. They desire to do what's
right before God and before others. Followers who are ethical
are careful with trade-offs. They have clear values and principled
behavior. They welcome accountability, they report both good news
and bad news, they avoid cheating, stealing, manipulating others, and
stretching the truth. They are concerned for doing what is good, just,
and right. They want all people to be treated fairly.

Noah is an example of a follower in the Bible that had a reputation
for being ethical. He desired to do what was right before God and also
before others. He was regarded as being blameless among the people
(Genesis 6:9). Being blameless among all the people is a sure sign of
someone who has been principled in all of his dealings.

Selected Passages related to being Ethical

*We are careful to be honorable before the Lord, but we
also want everyone else to see that we are honorable.* 2
Corinthians 8:21

*But now you must be holy in everything you do, just as
God who chose you is holy.* 1 Peter 1:15

*Don't be concerned for your own good but for the good
of others.* 1 Corinthians 10:24

Because we have these promises, dear friends, let us cleanse ourselves from everything that can defile our body or spirit. And let us work toward complete holiness because we fear God. 2 Corinthians 7:1

Who may worship in your sanctuary, Lord? Who may enter your presence on your holy hill? Those who lead blameless lives and do what is right, speaking the truth from sincere hearts. Those who refuse to gossip or harm their neighbors or speak evil of their friends. Those who despise flagrant sinners, and honor the faithful followers of the Lord, and keep their promises even when it hurts. Psalm 15:1-4

Don't copy the behavior and customs of this world, but let God transform you into a new person by changing the way you think. Then you will learn to know God's will for you, which is good and pleasing and perfect. Romans 12:2

And now, dear brothers and sisters, one final thing. Fix your thoughts on what is true, and honorable, and right, and pure, and lovely, and admirable. Think about things that are excellent and worthy of praise. Philippians 4:8

So let's not get tired of doing what is good. At just the right time we will reap a harvest of blessing if we don't give up. Therefore, whenever we have the opportunity, we should do good to everyone—especially to those in the family of faith. Galatians 6:9-10

It is God's will that your honorable lives should silence those ignorant people who make foolish accusations against you. 1 Peter 2:15

Because we belong to the day, we must live decent lives for all to see. Don't participate in the darkness of wild parties and drunkenness, or in sexual promiscuity and immoral living, or in quarreling and jealousy. Romans 13:13

Yet true godliness with contentment is itself great wealth. After all, we brought nothing with us when we came into the world, and we can't take anything with us when we leave it. So if we have enough food and clothing, let us be content. 1 Timothy 6:6-8

Don't love money; be satisfied with what you have. For God has said, "I will never fail you. I will never abandon you." Hebrews 13:5

Authentic. Those who follow well are authentic at all times with others. This means they are genuine, humble, and always viewing other people as people. They view others as beings that bear the image of God. Those who follow well are humble and aware of their own motives. They respect other followers. They respect the leader. They are self- disclosing and straightforward. They connect with people easily. They are not aloof or proud. They try not to view people as objects. They don't lord it over other followers. They don't project a false front or become overly concerned with image management. They're not self-deceived.

Nathaniel is a good example of authenticity. When Jesus first met Nathaniel, he exclaimed, "Now here is a genuine son of Israel—a man of complete integrity" (John 1:47). Authentic followers are genuine and humble. They want to be pure in heart.

Selected Passages related to being Authentic

The sacrifice you desire is a broken spirit. You will not reject a broken and repentant heart, O God. Psalm 51:17

How can I know all the sins lurking in my heart? Cleanse me from these hidden faults. Psalm 19:12

My old self has been crucified with Christ. It is no longer I who live, but Christ lives in me. So I live in this earthly body by trusting in the Son of God, who loved me and gave himself for me. Galatians 2:20

No, O people, the Lord has told you what is good, and this is what he requires of you: to do what is right, to love mercy, and to walk humbly with your God. Micah 6:8

Because of the privilege and authority God has given me, I give each of you this warning: Don't think you are better than you really are. Be honest in your evaluation of yourselves, measuring yourselves by the faith God has given us. Romans 12:3

Don't be selfish; don't try to impress others. Be humble, thinking of others as better than yourselves. Philippians 2:3

Respect everyone, and love your Christian brothers and sisters. Fear God, and respect the king. 1 Peter 2:17

In the same way, you younger men must accept the authority of the elders. And all of you, serve each other in humility, for "God opposes the proud but favors the humble." 1 Peter 5:5

Love each other with genuine affection, and take delight in honoring each other. Romans 12:10

Let everyone see that you are considerate in all you do. Remember, the Lord is coming soon. Philippians 4:5

Understand this, my dear brothers and sisters: You must all be quick to listen, slow to speak, and slow to get angry. James 1:19

Finally, all of you should be of one mind. Sympathize with each other. Love each other as brothers and sisters. Be tenderhearted, and keep a humble attitude. 1 Peter 3:8

Work at living in peace with everyone, and work at living a holy life, for those who are not holy will not see the Lord. Hebrews 12:14

Do all that you can to live in peace with everyone. Romans 12:18

Loving. Good followers consistently show love towards other people and towards the leader. The Bible is filled with verses teaching the importance of love and commanding us to love others. A loving follower is one who loves God and loves his neighbor as himself. Those who follow well treat other people as they would like to be treated themselves. They are kind and forgiving. They are generous towards others, and look for ways to serve their neighbor. Because of love, a good follower will submit to the leader and other followers. Loving followers are not caustic, touchy, or irritable. They are not cold, impersonal, or intolerant. They handle conflict and tension well without overreacting, and they don't hold grudges and are not self-centered.

Because our God is relational, we should view leadership as establishing a relationship with followers and leading in the context of a relationship. As we lead, we should remember that we are not merely influencing people or just telling them what to do, but we are establishing a relationship of trust with followers. This requires true love for them. Though we may be lacking, we can ask God to fill our heart with love so that we can love our followers deeply just as God loves those who follow him (Ephesians 5:1-2).

John is a good example of a follower who exhibited true love. The book of 1 John is filled with encouragement to love one another. He lived longer than any of the other disciples and continued to grow in love. Similarly, there will always be room in our heart to grow in love toward those who lead us.

Selected Passages related to being Loving

And you must love the Lord your God with all your heart, all your soul, and all your strength. Deuteronomy 6:5

"Teacher, which is the most important commandment in the law of Moses?" Jesus replied, "You must love the Lord your God with all your heart, all your soul, and all your mind." Matthew 22:36-37

And now, Israel, what does the Lord your God require of you? He requires only that you fear the Lord your God, and live in a way that pleases him, and love him and serve him with all your heart and soul. And you must always obey the Lord's commands and decrees that I am giving you today for your own good. Deuteronomy 10:12-13

If someone says, "I love God," but hates a Christian brother or sister, that person is a liar; for if we don't love people we can see, how can we love God, whom we cannot see? 1 John 4:20

And may the Lord make your love for one another and for all people grow and overflow, just as our love for you overflows. 1 Thessalonians 3:12

But the Holy Spirit produces this kind of fruit in our lives: love, joy, peace, patience, kindness, goodness, faithfulness, gentleness, and self-control. There is no law against these things! Galatians 5:22-23

In view of all this, make every effort to respond to God's promises. Supplement your faith with a generous provision of moral excellence, and moral excellence with knowledge, and knowledge with self-control, and self-control with patient endurance, and patient endurance with godliness, and godliness with brotherly affection, and brotherly affection with love for everyone. 2 Peter 1:5-7

Above all, clothe yourselves with love, which binds us all together in perfect harmony. Colossians 3:14

Dear friends, let us continue to love one another, for love comes from God. Anyone who loves is a child of God and knows God. 1 John 4:7

But we don't need to write to you about the importance of loving each other, for God himself has taught you to love one another. 1 Thessalonians 4:9

Love is patient and kind. Love is not jealous or boastful or proud. 1 Corinthians 13:4

This is my commandment: Love each other in the same way I have loved you. John 15:12

Most important of all, continue to show deep love for each other, for love covers a multitude of sins. 1 Peter 4:8

Since God chose you to be the holy people he loves, you must clothe yourselves with tenderhearted mercy, kindness, humility, gentleness, and patience. Colossians 3:12

Don't just pretend to love others. Really love them. Hate what is wrong. Hold tightly to what is good. Romans 12:9

You must be compassionate, just as your Father is compassionate. Luke 6:36

Do not seek revenge or bear a grudge against a fellow Israelite, but love your neighbor as yourself. I am the Lord. Leviticus 19:18

For the whole law can be summed up in this one command: "Love your neighbor as yourself." Galatians 5:14

Do to others whatever you would like them to do to you. This is the essence of all that is taught in the law and the prophets. Matthew 7:12

Here are some questions that can help good followers become more REAL:

Responsible: am I being a responsible person while keeping appropriate boundaries? Am I taking initiative without taking over?

Ethical: am I doing what's right while balancing multiple demands in my life? Am I treating people fairly but also getting the job done?

Authentic: Am I being my true self at all times without making it all about me? Can I experience a little success without losing humility?

Loving: Do I love my leaders and other followers as I love myself? Do I show love to problematic people without ignoring my effectiveness as a follower?

Followership Never Ends

We might as well learn to follow well because we will be followers the rest of our lives. Even when we hold a leadership position, we will still report to a manager or a board of directors and must follow their directives. When we work with any team where individuals have roles based on expertise, there are times when certain members will temporarily lead the way. If we are good leaders we share leadership, meaning that we do a lot of following as we lead. Even if we act as an absolute dictator at work and never follow anyone or take their advice, we have other roles in other areas of life where we are the follower.

Those who can't or won't follow well are not "natural leaders" or "alpha males." They are not "strong leaders." They are leaders who use and abuse power. They are control freaks. They are people with severe character flaws. They need to get REAL.

As we grow in our ability to follow well, we also grow in our ability to lead. This is because leadership and followership are two sides of the same coin. To lead well we need to understand the leader-follower dynamic as God created it. To create the conditions for that dynamic to occur, we need to follow well and help others follow well. The best leaders are also the best followers.

The essence of leadership is helping people follow well.

Session One: The Story

1. When you think back to the story, what were some of your favorite parts? What intrigued you?

2. Which character in the story did you most identify with, and why?

3. In what ways did this story impact you or lead you to significant insights?

4. What was the most surprising insight you learned about the theology of leadership and followership?

5. In many places in the New Testament, Jesus said, "Follow me" (Matthew 4:19, 8:22, 9:9, 16:24, 19:21; Mark 1:17, 2:14, 8:34, 10:21; Luke 5:27, 9:23, 9:59, 14:27, 18:22; John 1:43, 10:27, 12:26, 21:19). What is the significance of Jesus' question? What does this phrase mean to you now?

Session Two: Your Story

1. Who do you consider to be a great leader from history? Why is this person significant to you?

2. Who have been good role models of leadership in your life? What was it about them as a leader or as a person that made them effective?

3. When was a time when you experienced mistreatment from a leader that you would classify as follower abuse? How did this experience impact you?

4. Read 2 Timothy 3:1-5. How does this passage relate to follower abuse? What would cause or allow leaders to act this way?

5. Do you tend to avoid or welcome opportunities to lead? To what degree is this related to bad leadership you have experienced in your lifetime?

Session Three: Failure and Transformation

1. What are some examples of well-known fallen or corrupt leaders who have been in the news? What do you think was the root cause of their failure?

2. Why won't simply "trying harder" guarantee success in someone wanting to become a better leader?

3. Saul, the king of Israel, hurled his spear at David so hard that the spear stuck in the wall as David dodged it (1 Samuel 19:10). What character flaws cause good leaders who lead well for a while to gradually go bad?

4. In what way can redemption and sanctification by grace through faith in Jesus improve someone's ability to lead apart from any leadership training?

5. Where do you most need God to change you to become a better follower and leader?

Session Four: Types of Followership

1. How would you explain the three types of leadership to someone who has not read the book?

2. In what way is this concept of Type I, Type II, and Type III followership helpful to you?

3. When have you observed a leader or follower confusing the three types of followership?

4. Consider the life of David. See, for example, 1 Samuel 16:19-23, 17:12-15, 17:32-37, 18:5-11, 24:1-7, and Acts 13:22. How would you rate his followership in each of these three types?

5. What Type III leader-follower relationship do you need to renegotiate, and why?

Session Five: Levels of Followership

1. Name the roles in your life where you are following an individual or group. How would you rate your level of followership in each of those roles?

2. How would you describe the difference between level four and level five?

3. Why is level three less than ideal and under what circumstances might it be acceptable?

4. Who do you know who is a good example of following at level five? What does this person have that others lack? What specific behaviors demonstrate high-level followership?

5. Romans 12:8 says, "If God has given you leadership ability, take the responsibility seriously." In what situation might God be challenging you to express more of a leadership role?

Session Six: REAL Followership

1. Think of two very different people you know who represent a REAL follower. In what ways are they alike and in what ways are they different?

2. As you consider how well you follow others, which of the four aspects of being a REAL follower is most challenging to you currently?

3. Why is being responsible and taking responsibility so integral to good followership?

4. Joseph is a good example of REAL followership. How was he REAL when he served Potiphar (Genesis 39:1-6) and later the jailers in prison (Genesis 39:19-23)?

5. According to the apostle Paul, following exceptionally well, stepping up to take responsibility, being perfectly ethical and always being authentic and never fake, while failing to love others however, means you fall short. In 1 Corinthians 13:3, Paul talked about many excellent things he could be doing. Then he added, "But if I didn't love others, I would have gained nothing." What does it mean to show love to those who lead us?

Session Seven: The Leader-Follower Dynamic

1. When have you experienced the leader-follower dynamic occurring in an exceptionally effective way?

2. Why is this experience so fleeting and rare, in your opinion?

3. In what way can you see the leader-follower dynamic occurring in the story of Naomi and Ruth (Ruth 1:6-22)?

4. In what way can you see the leader-follower dynamic occurring in the story of David and Jonathan (1 Samuel 20:1-42)?

5. What specific actions can you take in one of your roles as a follower to help this dynamic to occur more often?

Session Eight: Your Followership and Leadership

1. What are some of the real costs for attempting to follow well?

2. When you find yourself not following well, what is typically getting in your way, both externally and internally?

3. Leadership and followership have a "doing" side and a "being" side. What do you observe about these two components in Psalm 78:72?

4. As a follower, what do you most need to work on? As a leader, what do you want to do differently as you lead?

5. Paul describes Jesus as emptying himself and giving up rights to everything he had the right to hold onto (Philippians 2:3:8). What rights, perks, privileges, titles, or attitudes do you need to let go of to make yourself available as a leader? What would it mean for you to empty yourself so that you can be prepared to lead well?

ABOUT THE AUTHOR

Jim Galvin is an organizational consultant specializing in strategic facilitation for a wide variety of organizations. For the past decade he has provided consulting and training in the areas of strategy formation, board governance, organizational change, and leadership development.

He has completed successful projects for the Prison Fellowship, Promise Keepers, Wycliffe Bible Translators, Youth for Christ, American Bar Association, National Guard, Department of Health and Human Services, Leadership Network, Willow Creek Association, Christian Leadership Alliance, Seacoast Church, Tyndale House Publishers, CareNet, World Relief, DeVos Foundation, and the Best Christian Workplaces Institute.

Jim is an award-winning author and he has written products published by Zondervan, Tyndale House, Thomas Nelson, Baker, Navpress, Moody Press, Intervarsity Press, Concordia, and Focus on the Family. He has won several ECPA Gold Medallion Awards as well as the C.S. Lewis Medal Award for Children's Literature. He is most well-known for his role as a co-creator of the widely-acclaimed *Life Application Study Bible*.

Jim holds the Doctor of Education degree in Curriculum and Instruction from Northern Illinois University as well as a B.A. and M.A. from Wheaton College in Christian Formation and Ministry. He and his wife Kathleen live in Elgin, Illinois. Their son Jimmy is an audio engineer and their daughter Lindsay is a graphic designer.

Contact information:
Email: jim@galvinandassociates.com
www.galvinandassociates.com

To order additional copies of *I've Got Your Back* and download a free discussion guide for this book, go to:

www.TenthPowerPublishing.com